Who can

Christianity and modern p
(Second edition)

F. G. HEROD
*Former Head of Religious Education Department,
Catford School*

Methuen Educational
London · Toronto · Sydney · Auckland

*By the same author
and published by Methuen Educational*

What Men Believe
The Life of Christ
(Secondary Certificate Questions series)
The Gospels: A First Commentary
Challenge!

Published by Hart Davis
World Religions

First published 1972
Reprinted six times
Second edition published 1981
by Methuen Educational
11 New Fetter Lane, London EC4P 4EE

©1972 and 1981 by F.G. Herod

All rights reserved.
No part of this publication may be
reproduced, stored in a retrieval system,
or transmitted in any form or by any means,
electronic, mechanical, photocopying,
recording or otherwise, without the prior
permission of the publisher.

Printed in Great Britain by
Fletcher & Son Ltd, Norwich

ISBN 0 423 50870 9

Contents

The chapters may be read in any order

You and Your world   *page* v
Family   *page* 1
World poverty   *page* 9
Money   *page* 18
Race   *page* 27
Work   *page* 38
War and violence   *page* 46
Leisure   *page* 55
Government   *page* 66
Sex and marriage   *page* 76
Religion   *page* 84
Examination Questions   *page* 95
Index   *page* 105

Acknowledgements

Thanks are due to the following for permission to use copyright material in this book:

Associated Press Ltd for the photograph appearing on p. 19

Camera Press Ltd for the photographs appearing on pp. 21, 24, 29, 34, 36, 39, 43, 48, 61, 68, 77, 81, 88. Also the photograph appearing on the cover.

Brian L. Davis for the photograph appearing on p. 2

Christopher Phillips for the photograph appearing on page 90.

Alfred Gregory for the photograph facing p. 1

The Israel Government Tourist Office for the photograph appearing on p. 3

Keystone Press Agency Ltd for the photographs appearing on pp. 22 and 58

Manchester City Council for the photograph appearing on p. 73

Canon D. Milmine for the photograph appearing on p. 53

Oxfam and Christian Aid for the photograph appearing on p. 11 and for the map on p. 12

Richard Bros, Penzance, for the photograph appearing on p. 49

Task Force for the photograph appearing on p. 62

Thanks are also due to Oxfam, Christian Aid and International Voluntary Service for permission to produce volunteer workers' letters; to the Jesus Movement for the detail from a poster, p. 94; and to the Examining Boards listed with the questions they have granted permission to publish.

A number of addresses will be found in the book of organisations willing to supply information, but each organisation would appreciate it if only one member of a class wrote to them on behalf of the others.

Cover photograph shows a black and white demonstration in California against the Vietnam war.

You and your world

'Our youth now love luxury. They have bad manners, contempt for authority . . . they contradict their parents, chatter before company, gobble up their food and tyrannize their teachers.'

Do you recognize yourselves? Is it true, half-true or merely the biased opinion that usually begins with 'When I was your age . . .'?

Should not the writer have added that many young people are dismayed by the state of the world in which they find themselves; impatient of their self-satisfied elders; and anxious to build by every means a more sensible society?

This book has been written in the belief that this is true.

The above quotation, incidentally, is a criticism of the youth of Athens by Plato in the fourth century B.C.

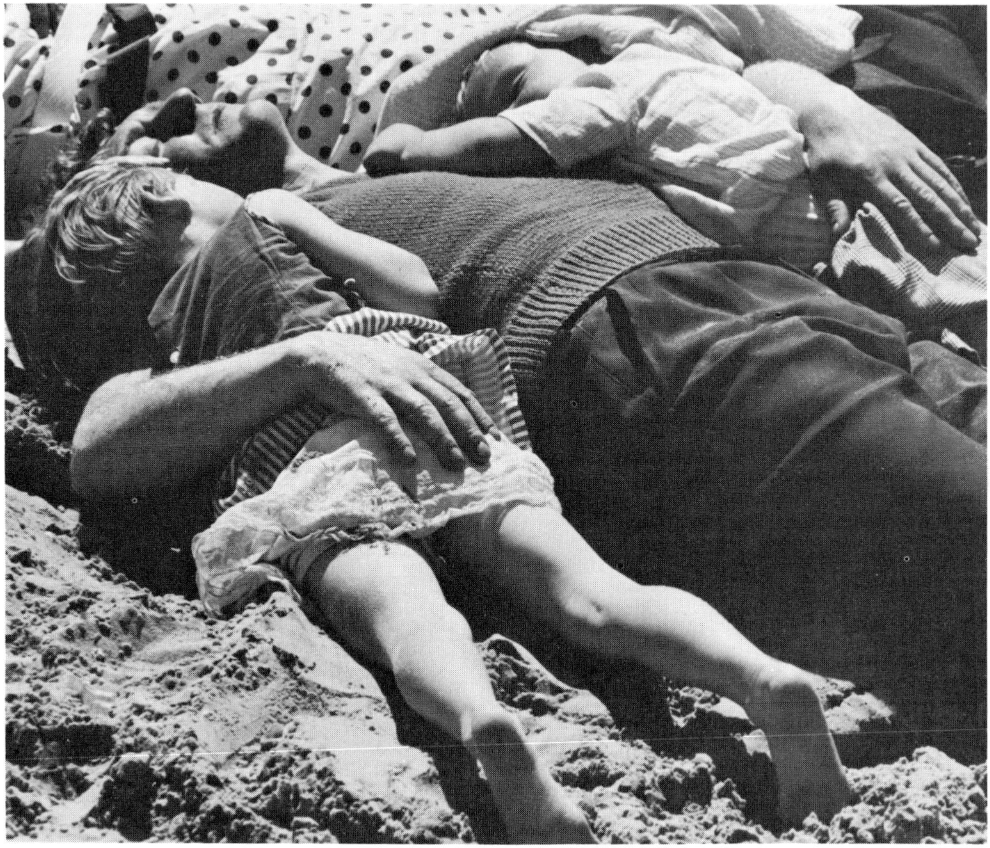

Family

One wise son can make his father glad;
forty fools avail him nothing.　　Hindu saying.

Children should never cause anxiety to their parents
except by unavoidable illness.　　Confucius

Be good to your parents.　　The Koran

He who honours his father shall have joy from his own children.　　Ecclesiasticus

Children, be obedient to your parents always; parents, never drive your children
to resentment or you will make them feel frustrated.　　Paul

He who spares the rod hates his own son.　　Proverbs

A parent should make no distinction between his own children.　　The Talmud

A man should spend less than his means on food and drink for himself, up to his
means on clothes, and above his means on honouring his wife and children.
The Talmud

Are parents the best people to rear their own children or has anyone ever found a better system?

Look up the word 'Spartan' in your dictionary. Its meaning will give you a clue to a very different system. In ancient Sparta puny and ill-shaped babies were not allowed to survive. They were left exposed in a mountain gorge to die. All boys at the age of seven were taken from their parents and brought up by the state.

There was no nonsense about mother-love in Sparta! The children were drilled unceasingly and put through a long hardening process which made them tough and skilful soldiers. If, for instance, they were caught stealing they were beaten, not for stealing, but for being clumsy enough to be found out.

In this century Hitler had similar ideas. The youth of Nazi Germany were trained in complete obedience. Hitler controlled their education and they were taught to be tough and brutal towards everyone who opposed the Nazi government. They were instructed to report family or friends whom they considered disloyal, and some of them as a result actually saw their own parents arrested and carried away to death in concentration camps.

[2] FAMILY

Russia in 1917 became a communist state. Children were ordered to disobey their parents if their demands were not in line with what the government required. But after eighteen years the experiment was abandoned, because it was felt that children who learnt to despise their parents soon learnt to despise all authority.

On p. 3 there is a picture of a settlement in Israel, called a kibbutz. When the Jews returned to Palestine they found so much hard work to be done to make the barren land fertile that they built these working settlements on the land. Today there are over two hundred of them. Everyone has to lend a hand, the women

Nazi youth

working alongside the men. So in many settlements the children are brought up in separate houses by teachers. This system seems to work fairly well, but in some settlements the children stay all day in crèches and sleep in their parents' homes at night.

Sparta, Russia, Germany, Israel — all are examples of how family life has been altered. But notice one thing. In each case it is the welfare of the state, not the children that comes first. If the children are to come first is there any alternative to family life as we know it? Can you think of one?

Keep in mind that psychologists insist that love and a sense of security are absolutely necessary in childhood. If for any reason these are missing, the child in later life may feel neither secure nor capable of real love himself. Judith Coleman quotes a striking example of this given by Margaret Mead, the anthropologist, who studied two tribes living quite close to each other. One of them, the Mundugumor tribe, put their children in wicker baskets immediately they were born and lifted them out only for feeding. The Arapesh tribe, on the other hand, kept their children close to their mothers' breasts for two years or more. The difference in these two tribes was remarkable. The Mundugumor were ferocious, aggressive and quarrelsome; the Arapesh gentle, generous and peaceloving.

Working on a Kibbutz

The human baby is one of the most helpless of all creatures and requires daily care, protection and guidance for many years. But for just how many years? This is one of the problems of the family system. It doesn't seem to exist among the lower animals. A young bird is pushed out of the nest and made to fend for itself as soon as it is able to do so. The parents want to be rid of their responsibility at the earliest possible moment. But in the human home the reverse is often true. Parents cling to control long after their children think it unnecessary.

'Who was that girl I saw you with at the end of the road?' demands Mum as

[4] FAMILY

soon as you walk in at the door. 'Turn that stereo down. Why must we have that din all night?' 'What do you want to wear that thing for?' 'See you're home by 9.30, won't you?'

Questions like these can be very annoying when all you want is to choose your own clothes, your own friends, your own pastimes and have a private life of your own. 'My mum says no to everything,' moaned one fourteen-year-old girl.

Of course, parents have their point of view. Newspapers and television give great publicity to missing children and the harm that sometimes comes to them. Rowdiness and crime among young people are on the increase. Parents naturally keep a close watch on what their children are doing and the company they keep.

Many parents, too, remember the mistakes they made when they were young and don't want their children to repeat them. So when it comes to the big decisions as, for example, whether to have that extra year or two at school, they are not impressed by such arguments as, 'Why should I stay at school and be treated like a kid when my friends have all left and are earning good money?' This surely is not a sensible attitude to a serious problem that may well affect the whole of your future life.

Are your parents, in fact, looking to you for just that — a sensible attitude to life — before they grant you more freedom of choice? Freedom cannot work in any society unless people think and act wisely.

Figures for juvenile crime show that it is most often the broken or unhappy home that produces the delinquent. Many children suffer from tragic home conditions. They find themselves uncared for or the miserable victims of parents' quarrels.

So, even if your parents moan a little and brothers or sisters get on your nerves, you may still be thankful. If you are fortunate enough to have a good home and the making of a real family spirit within it, work hard to preserve it. You are among the lucky ones of this generation.

Ann and Pauline have been looking forward to going to the cinema on Saturday evening to see a very popular film. But on Friday morning Ann, Pauline, Jennifer and Helen meet at 'break.'

Ann	Can't go on Saturday, Pauline.
Pauline	You've got to — you promised!
Ann	I know, but Mum won't let me. She's read something in the papers about it and says it's unsuitable.
Pauline	Unsuitable! She means it's a bit sexy, I suppose. I don't know how you

	get on at all. I'm lucky. My Mum never bothers as long as she knows where I'm going and what time I'm coming in. . . . . . . Well, I can't go alone. Can you come, Jennifer?
Jennifer	You must be joking! You know my Dad won't let me out of his sight since that row over Pete. He goes mad if he thinks I'm out with a boy.
Pauline	Well, you won't be out with a boy.
Jennifer	More's the pity! But he won't believe it. Every time I was out with Pete, I was supposed to be out with you. My Mum's on his side too. I could hate them sometimes. I'm fed up with their moaning.
Helen	It's your own fault. You shouldn't tell lies. They always find out. Mine do.
Ann	You're lucky. Your Mum invites your boy friends in.
Jennifer	I wish she'd invite my Dad in and tell him how to trust his little Jenny! He still thinks I'm seven.
Helen	Funny, that. My Dad's the same — stricter than my Mum. Anyway, I'd rather have them strict than don't care. It's for your own good in the end, you know.
Ann	If you lived with my Nan you wouldn't say that. She's only got to look at me to know what I'm thinking and she's always nagging me to wash-up, clean the house, run here and there to save my Mum's legs. She's always on at me. I just walk out of the room.
Pauline	Well, what about tomorrow night?
Ann / Helen / Jennifer	Sorry.
Pauline	Oh well, I can't go then.
Ann	I'm really sorry, Pauline. What about coming round to our house and playing cards with my Nan. She likes you.

1. Do you think Ann's mother was right in not letting her see the film? Why?
2. What advantage is there in being able to take your boy-friend (girl-friend) home?
3. Who was to blame for Jennifer being kept at home?
4. Is it ever right not to tell your parents the truth about what you are doing when you are out?
5. 'I'd rather have them strict than don't care.' Do you agree with Helen?
6. 'She's always nagging me.' It sounds as if Ann might do a little more to help in the house, at least her Nan thinks so. What do you think about helping at home?

[6] FAMILY

If you should ever call at a Jewish home, you might see fastened to the doorpost at the entrance a small cylinder or box. It is called a Mezuzah. It contains fifteen verses of scripture inscribed minutely on a scroll. A Jew, as he enters his home, touches it with his finger. This is a sign that he regards his home as sacred to God.

Synagogue and home are equally sacred in Jewish eyes. Within the home the family are brought close together by their religious faith. Festivals are celebrated there, and every Friday evening special prayers are said over a candle-lit supper table.

As a consequence the Jews set a fine example to the world in their home life, their faithfulness in marriage and their care of children and old people. Even in their present-day experiment, the Kibbutzim, there is practically no trace among their young people of violence, drug taking, excessive drinking or sex before marriage.

Jesus, therefore, in his day would not meet serious problems about the relationship of parents and children. There would be, of course, the exceptions. We can find examples in the Old Testament: rebelliousness (David and Absalom 2 Samuel, 15–18), treachery (David and Bathsheba 2 Samuel 11), favouritism (Rebecca and Jacob Genesis 27). But generally Jesus would not feel it necessary to say a great deal on this subject.

"Then he went back to Nazareth and continued to be under their authority." This was Jesus at twelve years old, after being lost for four days and found by his parents in the Temple. All the record adds about his boyhood is 'As Jesus grew up, he advanced in wisdom and in favour with God and man.'

Later in life, as a teacher, he has some strong words to say on divorce and unfaithfulness in marriage. He stresses more than once the fifth Commandment: 'Honour your father and your mother,' and has some acid comments on rabbis who twist the law to make it legal for a man to neglect his parents. He shows a deep love for children and is angry with his disciples when they think that he is either too important or too busy to give them his blessing. During the final agony of death he remembers his mother and asks John, his disciple, to look after her. Apart from this he says little directly about the family.

What Jesus believed in he would find in most families: a faith in God and the rules of conduct that go with it. What he taught was that true love and humility, as shown for example in the story of the Prodigal Son, can solve most family problems.

FAMILY [7]

Passages from the Bible for further study

Luke 2, 41–50	An example of disobedience
Luke 2, 51	An example of obedience
Mark 10, 13–16	Children are
Matt. 18, 1–6	very important
Ephesians 4, 32	The right
I Corinthians 12, 13–27	family spirit
Ephesians 6, 1–4	Parent–child
Exodus 20, 12	relations
Proverbs 23, 22	Looking after
John 19, 26–27	one's parents
Luke 15, 11–32	Two brothers and their father
Mark 7, 9–13	How to avoid honouring
Matt. 15, 4–6	one's parents.

For Discussion

1. What do you think about the following statements:
    a: 'I don't tell anyone at home where I am going or what time I shall be be in.' 14 year old boy.
    b: 'I don't want any advice, thank you. I want to learn from my own mistakes.' 18 year old girl leaving school.
    c: 'I think one's parents ought to help out!' young married daughter with money troubles.
2. Read the quotations at the beginning of the chapter. Which, if any, do you disagree with and why?
3. Write down
    a: six things you enjoy for nothing through being a member of your family
    b: six things you do voluntarily to help in the home.
4. What mistakes would you like to avoid when you become a parent yourself?
5. If parental influence is very important what do you think about
    a: mothers using nursery schools?
    b: young children being sent to boarding school?

[8] FAMILY

6. Robert Browning wrote:
   'Grow old along with me. The best is yet to be:
   The last of life for which the first was made.'
   The 'last of life' should be as happy and rewarding as the earlier part. What are the difficulties of old age and how should family life cope with them?
7. Write a play consisting of one scene, entitled 'A Spot of Bother' which features a family row. Write
   a: the scene as you think it would take place
   then
   b: the scene as you think it ought to take place in order to avoid the row.
8. Discuss the family problems that lie behind the following statements:
   a: 'I can't talk to my dad'
   b: 'Every time my young sister passes me she kicks me'
   c: 'Mum, why haven't you cleaned my shoes?'
   d: 'Put the other programme on, Barry. I want to see the News.'
9. Every organisation must have rules. Write down up to a dozen rules that could make a home run smoothly.
10. Experiments in community instead of family life are always interesting. The Israeli settlements are amongst the best of them. Find out what you can about them and give a five-minute talk to the class on the subject. The Jewish Agency, Rex House, 4 Regent Street, London, S.W.1 will supply information on the Kibbutzim.

World poverty

Give even though you have but little to give.   Buddhist saying

*People give according to their faith
or according to their pleasure.*   Buddhist saying

When I was hungry, you gave me food; when thirsty, you gave me drink; when I was a stranger you took me into your home, when naked you clothed me; when I was ill you came to my help, when in prison you visited me.   Jesus

*Blessed is he who also fasts for this,
that he might feed the poor.*   Early Christian saying

When the poor are roughly turned away from your gate, they carry off your good deeds with them, and upon you lay their sins.   Hindu saying

The more charity, the more peace.   Jewish saying

True charity is practised in secret. The best type of charity is where the person who gives does not know who receives it; and the person who receives it does not know who gives it.   Jewish saying

*He is not a perfect Muslim who eats his fill
and lets his neighbour go hungry.*   Mohammed

How would you care to live on a diet of rice pudding every day of your life? Three people out of four in the world exist in this way.

> *Three-quarters of mankind in essence know only one dish, a basic food (bread, rice, cassava, maize, millet, etc.) flavoured by a sauce of some kind*   (UNESCO)

so that almost every time they sit down to a meal the same dreary diet faces them.

If it does not contain the food necessary for sound health, they grow up sickly and weak, liable to catch diseases and to die earlier than they should. They are suffering from what is called malnutrition. Half the people in the world suffer from malnutrition either for the whole of life or part of it.

Some parts of the world are much worse off than others. India, for example, can produce only enough food to feed two-thirds of her population. This means that millions of people in India are slowly starving to death because there is just not enough food to go round.

[10] WORLD POVERTY

The world therefore is divided into "the haves" and "the have-nots". The average Englishman is fifteen times better off than the average Indian; the American, thirty times better off. In the west we have food enough and to spare — in fact, to waste, judging by the contents of our dustbins. And the people of the underdeveloped countries are becoming more aware of it every year.

This then is problem No. 1 for mankind, for at the present growth rate, the population of the world will have doubled by the year 2000.

A computer analysis from the Institute of Technology, Massachusetts, gave a very gloomy view of the future. It declared that the human race faced starvation unless, *within the next few years,*

    a: we stabilized the world population

    b: we used all possible arable land and learned to enrich and preserve it

    c: we were prepared to accept a modest standard of life instead of continually seeking a higher one.

In 1980, ex-prime minister Edward Heath and ex-West German chancellor Willy Brandt, in a joint statement, gave a further warning of the certainty of world disaster unless we tackled the appalling gap between the rich and poor countries of the world.

    1:    The number of quotations at the beginning of this chapter could easily have been doubled. Every religion makes an important point of giving to the poor. Why is this?

    2:    'When you do some act of charity, do not let your left hand know what your right hand is doing.' Find the Jewish saying which expresses the same idea. Why is this 'true charity?'

The late John F Kennedy, once president of the United States, believed that by united international effort in this generation we could end thirst and hunger in the world and conquer poverty and disease. Was he right? Is it possible that the 'population explosion' will cancel out all our efforts to solve these problems? Many governments today, especially in poor countries, are making great efforts to persuade their people to have smaller families. In this matter, since over half the adult population of the world can neither read nor write, the advance of education can help enormously.

But there is real hope elsewhere. Not many people know that mankind uses only one third of the earth's surface that could be cultivated. So that the amount of food grown could be three times what it is today.

Look at it another way:

    If the land of the world were evenly distributed each human being would have 12½ acres, four of them potentially cultivateable; he would cultivate one.

(Christian Aid)

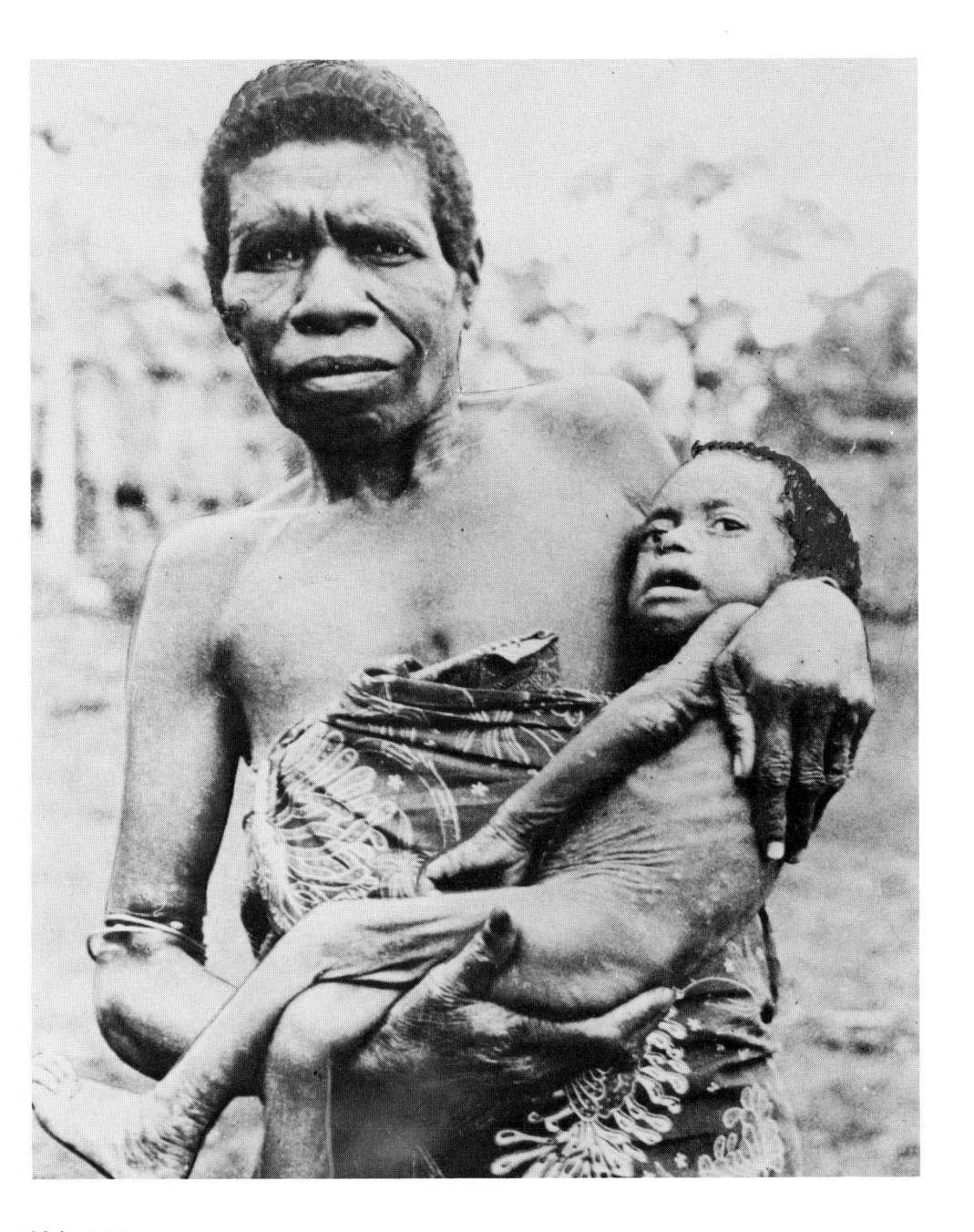

Malnutrition

[12] WORLD POVERTY

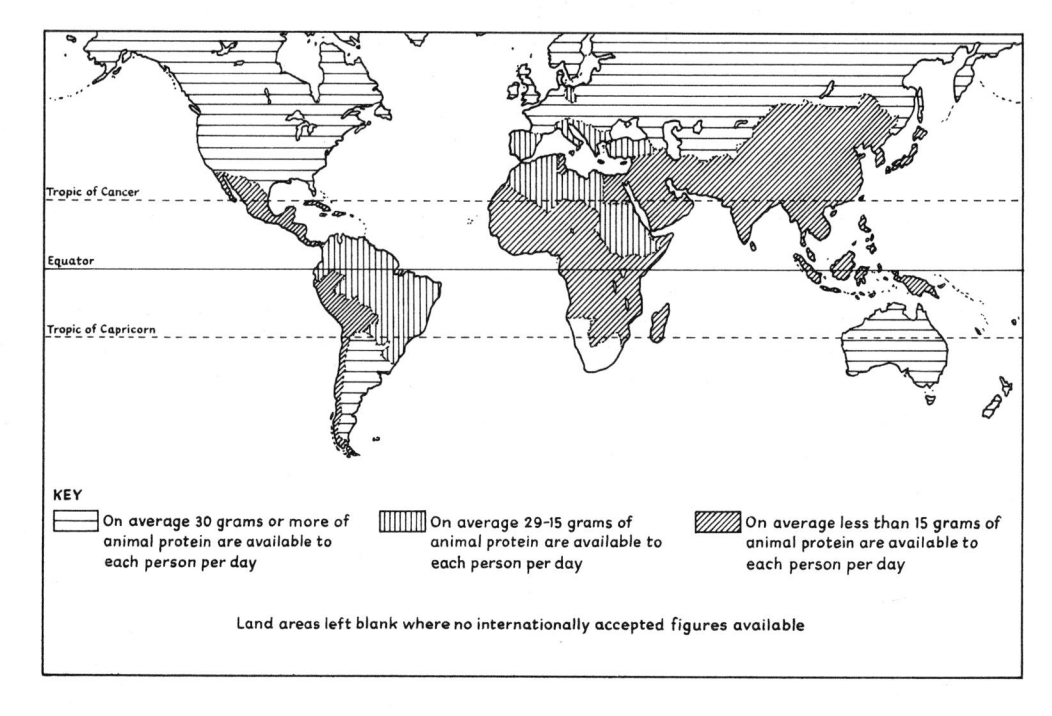

KEY
On average 30 grams or more of animal protein are available to each person per day
On average 29-15 grams of animal protein are available to each person per day
On average less than 15 grams of animal protein are available to each person per day

Land areas left blank where no internationally accepted figures available

Malnutrition

What is really needed then is a united effort of the human race to make the earth fruitful.

In this the Israelis have set us a fine example. When they took over Israel in 1948 it contained millions of acres of barren land. The Jews set to work living in their settlements on the land and toiling unceasingly to make the desert fertile. Today they are four times better off than their Arab neighbours.

If this experiment could be repeated thousands of times in other lands food could be plentiful. Of course, in order to succeed, the Jews had to have money, machines and technicians, but poor countries have none of these things and have found it difficult to make a start without outside help.

Such help is already being given in the following ways:

a: *By the United Nations.* Member states make an annual contribution and the money is used mainly to help with agriculture, education and health.

b: *By separate nations.* Britain, the United States, France and Russia, for example, have special interests in various parts of the world and provide money and skilled labour for development. Britain naturally gives and lends a great deal of money to Commonwealth countries (about £800 million a year).

c: *By voluntary organisations.* Such organisations as Oxfam and Christian Aid raise millions of pounds every year by collections. They will always find money to help in emergencies such as famine, earthquake and flood.

d: *By volunteer workers.* Every year many thousands of people from Britain and other countries go abroad to help in under-developed countries. They include school-leavers and students who give their services for two or three months or for longer periods up to one or two years. Work of every description is needed, both skilled and unskilled but the skilled worker with some experience behind him is wanted most of all. Board and accommodation are found and pocket money provided.

Here are extracts from some letters:
Graham Pearce spent two years in Lesotho working on a pineapple-growing scheme. He wrote

> *In my case, although I have always been interested in human relationships, I think the reason for my going to Africa was a rather selfish desire to be my own boss and do things my way, coupled with the ever present urge in most young people to see something of the world around them, especially a country as romantic as Africa.*
>
> *It wasn't until I had been there six months and had had time to see and digest at first hand some of the problems facing the African people that I developed the interest that I have now. It's a country that once under the skin stays there for good.*
>
> *The Pineapple project became an obsession with me and it wasn't long before I was generally known as Pineapple Pearce because of my incessant badgering for co-operation. . . .*
>
> *At the end of my two years I came away with a real sense of achievement and purpose, something I had never experienced before and probably won't again.*

Diana Chorley spent one year as an Oxfam-sponsored volunteer at the Amani Cheshire Home just outside Nairobi. There were twenty patients, ten adults and ten children, some paralysed, some deaf or blind, some spastic. All were incurables. She wrote,

> *Only one child can run around, but the rest move so fast in their wheelchairs that they are quite lethal. . . . My work around the Home is punctuated by singing, and chanting of multiplication tables, which is done with far more enthusiasm than accuracy. I am trying to get some percussion instruments to form a band. . . .*
>
> *Calamities happen each day. The electricity fails, the roof leaks. . . . So apart from being Sister, I am plumber, carpenter, electrician and as we have no permanent doctor I must prescribe drugs. I am also typist, and organiser of laundry, catering and staff.*
>
> *It's a great challenge working here. The need for Homes like ours is tremendous and I feel a bit of a pioneer.*

International Voluntary Service sent Barbara Hayes as a laboratory technician to McKean Leprosy Hospital, Chiengmai in Thailand. Barbara writes

> *This hospital already had a lab. before my arrival but it was staffed by patients, none of whom had any lab. science education. My job at present is to organise and supervise the lab., train the present staff and introduce further clinical tests. . . .*
>
> *The hospital is existing on an absolute minimum of staff and money but even if money was available, I think it would be impossible to get a qualified technician as the majority of Thais refuse to work with leprosy patients.*
>
> *Within the hospital the people seem poor but the people from the outside villages are in a desperate condition, especially healthwise as they receive no regular medical supervision. It is hoped next year to establish a team to visit these villages and to conduct survey work to find the undiagnosed cases as part of a programme for leprosy eradication. All this will mean a lot of extra work for the lab. both in organisation and in technical procedures so I think it will be a long time before a lab. technician at McKean finds there is little to do.*

Passages from the Bible for further study

Matt. 25, 31–46	Essential Christian service
Mark 6, 30–44	Concern for human needs
Luke 16, 19–31	The rich and the poor

WORLD POVERTY [15]

Luke 12, 16–21 — A pauper in the sight of God
James 2, 14–17 — Faith and works

For Discussion

1. No problem can be solved unless it is properly understood. This is a great opportunity for research work. Members of the class might write to the following organisations which are very co-operative, asking for information which would help to give an understanding of the problem of hunger. Then, working in groups, the class could discover for itself
   a: The distressed areas of the world
   b: The work of the U.N. in these areas
   c: The assistance being given by individual nations
   d: The Voluntary Societies' work
   e: The opportunities for working in these areas as a volunteer or on a more permanent basis

Organisations

United Nations Children's Fund	46 Osnaburgh Street, London NW1
War on Want	467 Caledonian Rd, London N7
Oxfam	274 Banbury Road, Oxford
Overseas Development Institute	10 Percy St, London W1
Centre for World Development and Education	128 Buckingham Palace Road, London SW1
Save the Children Fund	157 Clapham Rd, London SW9
Christian Aid	240 Ferndale Road, London SW9
Quaker Work Camps Committee	Friends' House, Euston Rd, London NW1
Ministry of Overseas Development	Eland House, Stag Place, London SW1
Christian Education Movement	Chester House, Pages Lane, London N10
Catholic Institute for International Relations	1 Cambridge Terrace, London NW1
United Nations Association	3 Whitehall Court, SW1
International Voluntary Service	82a Christchurch Road, SW2

[16] WORLD POVERTY

Action Aid 208 Upper Street, London N1
United Nations High Commissioner 36 Westminster Palace Gardens,
for Refugees Artillery Row, London SW1

2. The wealthy nations of the world help the poorer ones in different ways. They may give them what is called multilateral aid, which is aid that they contribute to a number of countries through such organisations as the World Bank. In 1977 30% of aid was given in this way.

   Bilateral aid, on the other hand, is that given by one government to another, e.g. Britain to India. It may be a loan which has to be repaid, usually with interest, or a grant that may be "tied". A tied grant is one that has to be spent by the government receiving it on goods from the donor country. This arrangement is rarely popular because the donor country fixes the prices which may well be higher than the poorer countries usually pay. Yet most bilateral aid is tied in this way.

   Some countries, however, have shown themselves to be generous. For example, Canada, Britain and Sweden have all written off the past debts of some very poor countries. Russia, on the other hand, insists on quite hard repayments and as a consequence gets more back in interest and capital than she gives out each year.

   The Gross National Product (GNP) of any country is the annual total value of the goods and services that it produces. The amount of aid given by various countries is compared by calculating it as a percentage of its GNP. Here are some recent figures given by "The Internationalist":

   USA .22%   CANADA .5%   USSR .03%
   UNITED KINGDOM .37%   AUSTRALIA .45%
   OPEC 2.65%

3. In the world today there are 800 million people living on the edge of starvation. There are 10 million homeless people. The situation is critical. Wayne Ellwood in an article in "The Internationalist" questions whether the kind of aid described above can alone solve the problem of world poverty. He makes three suggestions:
   a: Since poor nations are often forced, out of necessity, to sell their goods at a low price, the nations in the west should agree together to pay a fair market price for Third World produce.

WORLD POVERTY [17]

    b: That the tariffs raised against Third World goods, keeping them out of western markets, should be reduced.

    c: That rich countries should step up their programme for writing off the past debts of poorer nations.

4. Here are some actual comments on the problem of world poverty that might be discussed both before and after the class research:

    a: 'It's no good giving money — a lot of it doesn't even get there.'

    b: 'They're lazy. If they were willing to work they could get themselves out of this mess.'

    c: 'There are too many of them. If a million or so die, it will help.'

    d: 'We can't afford to help — we've too many problems of our own. We're nearly bankrupt!'

Money

How hard it will be for the wealthy to enter the Kingdom of God.   Jesus.

Be on your guard against greed of every kind, for even when a man has more than enough, his wealth does not give him life.   Jesus.

*Wealth is title to respect, fame and wisdom —
that it should be so is shame.*   Hindu saying.

*It is as hard to be poor without complaining
as to be rich without becoming arrogant.*   Confucius.

He who multiplies property multiplies worries.   Jewish Mishnah.

*Wealth, properly employed is a blessing,
and one may lawfully endeavour to increase it by honest means.*   Mohammed.

I have learned in whatsoever state I am, therewith to be content.   Paul.

Here are a number of different ways in which people look at money.

Bank Robbery   Three masked men, armed with pickaxe handles, burst into the bank in Russell St. this morning ten minutes after opening time. Vaulting over the counter, they ransacked the tills, getting away with about £8000. A customer who tried to intercept one of them was violently attacked and was later reported in hospital to be still unconscious. The men escaped in a waiting Jaguar later found abandoned.

'Bank Robbery', 'Wages Snatch,' 'Elderly Shopkeeper Battered to Death'. Items like these in the newspaper seem hardly worth a passing glance. We are so used to them.

There has always been robbery with violence. In times of war whole nations have sometimes been involved in it. The terrible urge to get rich at any cost causes men to risk life and limb and to maim and murder one another.

Very many other people who would not act violently nevertheless put money first in life. 'I want to make a lot of money and spend it on myself,' declared a

Bank robbery photographed by a hidden camera

student recently. Twelve of them were interviewed by the magazine *The Queen*. Out of nine men six said that their aim in life was to get a lot of money. 'I want to make a lot of money in order to satisfy my very expensive tastes,' said another. 'I want to live and be seen to live as a rich man,' said a third.

Unfortunately, there are many ways other than physical violence of harming our fellowmen. People who have this tremendous passion to get money are not always concerned to know exactly how it is made. Huge fortunes and vast estates have been built up in most countries at the expense of the health and happiness of countless people. Paul, a great traveller in the Roman Empire, gave it as his opinion that 'the love of money is the root of all evil.' Certainly it has provoked almost every sin known to man. And the result throughout man's history has remained much the same: the privileged few have enjoyed great wealth and the masses have remained poor.

In modern times conditions have improved, yet the distribution of wealth still remains very uneven. In Britain 10% of the population owns 75% of the private wealth of the country (Parliamentary Answer, October 1970). And in rich countries like Britain and America millions of people are still homeless or living in

[20] MONEY

houses 'unfit for human habitation', and many still die of neglect and semi-starvation.

1. Give any examples you can think of where the pursuit of money has caused or is causing suffering.
2. What is meant by cut-throat competition? How does it affect the people concerned in it?
3. Which quotations at the head of this chapter suggest that it is not only the poor who suffer in the scramble for wealth?

A different attitude to money was shown by a girl student. 'I want money so that I don't have to worry about it,' she said. Many people would settle for that happy state of affairs. The real problem arises when we ask ourselves just how much money is 'enough.' People's wants are greater today than ever before.

This is certainly true of teenagers because there is so much more to buy. Your parents, when they were your age, had none of the following: colour TV, hi-fi, video recorders, cassettes, electronic games and calculators, instamatic cameras and discos.

There is, of course, more money to spend. The average wage in 1938 for a boy of eighteen was £1; for a girl 92½p. Today, the corresponding figures are £43.70 and £36.40, which, allowing for the increased cost of living, are double those of forty years ago.

Yet there are greater temptations to spend because advertising has become a fine art. In America, according to Vance Packard in *The Hidden Persuaders*, millions of dollars are spent in discovering exactly the right way to advertise goods so that people cannot resist buying them. Advertisers even employ psychiatrists to probe people's minds in depth to discover what particular angle will succeed. The results are amazingly successful.

In Britain, also, enormous sums are spent on advertising. One single full-page advertisement in a national newspaper can cost about £11,000. And on every hand — newspapers, magazines, hoardings, neon signs, cinemas, television, radio — you are being skilfully bombarded with ideas for spending your money.

Add to this the strange urge some people have 'to keep up with the Jones's' and the ease with which they can begin hire-purchase payments on expensive articles which they cannot really afford, and 'enough' means, in fact, a very great deal.

Statistics show that there are many people under these pressures who get badly into debt, and that keeping up payments causes them constant worry and discontent.

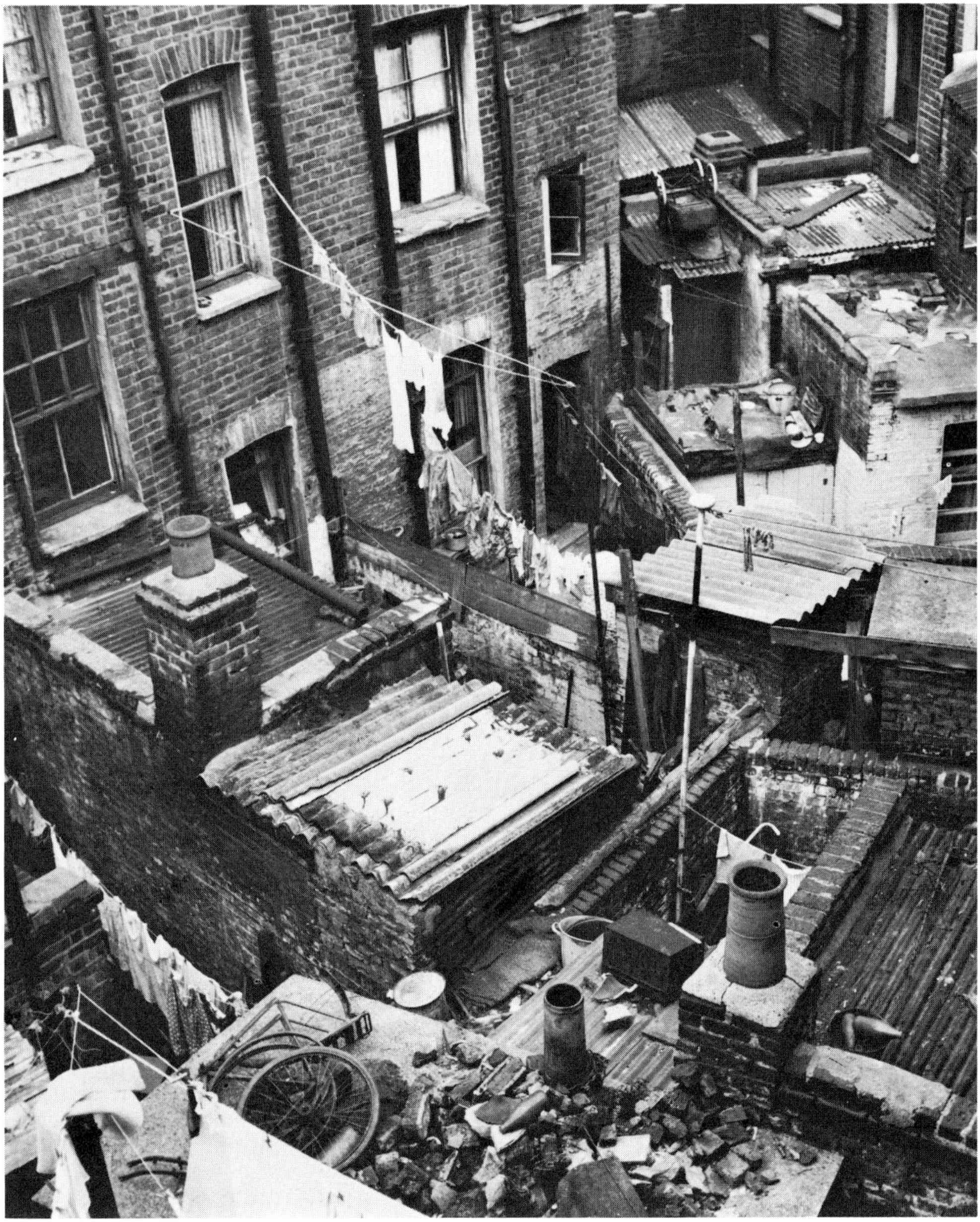

[22] MONEY

Perhaps you can think of a more sensible way of living. Mohammed, you may remember, said 'Wealth properly employed is a blessing,' and that surely is what God intended it to be.

> Write down half a dozen or more advertisements that you can remember. Each has its special line of appeal. Can you find it? Does it, for example, appeal to
> 1. the desire to appear manly?
> 2. the desire to be femininely attractive?
> 3. the desire for glamour and romance?
> 4. the desire to appear well-off?
> 5. the desire to appear refined and to have good taste?
>
> Can you think of advertisements where a well-known person is used to recommend the goods or where doctors, nurses or other professional people are connected in some way with the advertisement to add weight to it? Can you think of advertisements that appeal to some emotion such as fear or greed?

Here, finally, is a completely different attitude. Fritz Kreisler was one of the most brilliant violinists of the twentieth century. He could have been a very wealthy man but he and his wife lived quite simply and gave most of his money away. He explained, 'People do not understand just why we do not feel that we have any right to spend money carelessly. It is very simple. We feel that we are stewards of my talent and the money that comes from it. It is God's gift and we are its stewards.'

The Kreislers were Christians and extremely happy people. Whether we share their beliefs or not, there is one interesting point about their way of life that we should note. They lived a simple life and enjoyed it. Their personal wants were few and yet they were content.

We, however, are born into an acquisitive society. This means that from an early age we are brought up to want things. As individuals and as nations we tend to think that the more we have, the happier we shall be. But is it really true? Jesus said, 'Even when a man has more than enough, his wealth cannot give him life.' Could we not, in fact, be much more content if we trained ourselves to value and enjoy a little more the things we already possess?

Buddha taught that all the evil and unhappiness in life arises simply from wanting things. Get rid of your desires, he said, and you will be happy. This may seem an extreme statement but is there not some point in the following conversation between Pyrrhus, the ancient soldier king, and a philosopher friend about his future plans?

'First', said Pyrrhus, 'I shall conquer Italy.'
'What will you do after that?'
'Then I shall take Sicily.'
'And then?'
'I shall conquer Greece and Macedonia.'
'And after that?'
'Carthage, I think.'
'And then?'
'Oh,' said Pyrrhus, 'then we can settle down and enjoy what we have won.'
'But why,' replied his friend, 'can't you settle down now and begin to enjoy what you already have, without all this fighting?'

'The simple life': a youth commune in Friesland

Passages from the Bible for further study

Mark 10, 17–30 \} Luke 18, 18–30	What hope is there for the rich?
Luke 12, 13–21	The rich man who was a pauper.
Mark 12, 41–44 \} Luke 21, 1–4	Poverty and generosity.
Luke 20, 21–25	The rival claims of the state and religion.
Matt. 6, 19–34	Why worry when you can pray?
Luke 16, 1–8	When dishonesty pays.
Matt. 20, 1–15	"Unto this last".
Luke 16, 19–31	The responsibility of being rich.
Luke 19, 1–10	How Christ affects a rich man.
Acts 2, 41–47	Christian Communism.

For Discussion

1. What are the advantages of being well-off?
2. What is meant by the quotation, 'He who multiplies property multiplies worries?' Do you think that there are any other dangers in being rich? Consider, for example, the man who wins £10,000 from the football pools.
3. Make a list of six things you can really enjoy that cost nothing or very little. Do you make the most of them?
4. Recently it was reported that £10,000 was spent on a coming-out party, and £3000 on a wedding reception. Do you think that spending money on this scale is justified today? Is spending money 'like water' anti-social or should we take the view that a man has a right to do what he likes with his own money?
5. Christians are expected to give regularly to the Church and to good causes. Some tithe themselves for this purpose. Muslims are required to give 2½% of their income to support the poor in their community. There are many organisations and institutions that depend on public subscriptions to carry on their work, for example, the N.S.P.C.C., Children's Homes and Orphanages, and Christian Aid. (Can you think of others?)

[26] MONEY

When we are earning ought we to set aside an amount regularly to give away in some direction or other?

6. Is it a good plan to save regularly when you are young? If so, for what? What are the best ways of saving money?
7. John Wesley said, 'Earn all you can; save all you can; give all you can.' Is this a good maxim?
8. When you start work will you expect to pay your parents if you live at home
    a: less than it costs to keep you
        or
    b: exactly what it costs to keep you
        or
    c: more than it costs to keep you?
9. If you marry and have a family will you expect
    a: the wife to take the wages, pay all the bills and allot spending money to her husband
        or
    b: the husband to control the expenditure and give his wife an allowance for housekeeping and personal expenses
        or
    c: take a joint responsibility for everything, regularly discussing your budget together?

    Each system has advantages. What are they?
10. What are the advantages and disadvantages of hire purchase? 'I make a point of never having more than one thing at a time on H.P.' Do you think this is a good rule? If not, how would you modify it?
11. Have you ever been misled by advertisements and bought something which did not match up to the claims made for it? Describe your experience.
12. Make a budget for your weekly spending as though you had already begun work. If you don't know what you will earn, use one of the average figures for teenagers given in this chapter.

Race

All men are brothers;
all receive the blessings of the same heaven.   Shinto saying.

Do you love your Creator? Then love your fellowmen first. All God's children are his family, and he is most beloved of God who does most good to his creatures. Mohammed.

Have we not all one Father? Has not one God created us all?   Jewish saying.

A man should treat all creatures in the world
as he himself would like to be treated.   Jain saying.

You shall love your neighbour as yourself.   Jesus.

He has made of one blood all nations of men.   Paul.

Look at the map [on p. 28]. It gives you the names of the principal races of mankind and shows you where they lived before man became civilized and began to travel widely. There are five of them. Their names may be unfamiliar, but see if you can recognise them from the following descriptions (as given in *Towards International Co-operation* by Sulwyn Lewis).

- a: *The Caucasoid:* pale white to light brown skin, wavy, curly or straight hair, narrow nose. The males may have much body hair.
- b: *The Mongoloid:* yellowish or yellow-brown skin, coarse black head hair, brown eyes, prominent cheek-bones, little body hair and generally a fold in the upper eye-lid.
- c: *The Negro:* black skin, woolly or kinky head hair, broad, flat nose, small ears, thick lips, little body hair.
- d: *The American Indian:* brown or reddish skin, similar in other respects to Mongoloid with a less developed upper eye-lid fold, and a more prominent, convex nose.
- e: *The Australoid:* brown skin, wavy or curly hair, broad nose, receding chin and brow ridges. Facial and body hair similar in amount to Caucasoid.

It is very important that we should learn as much about the races of mankind as possible. A century ago it would not have mattered at all, because 'foreigners'

[28] RACE

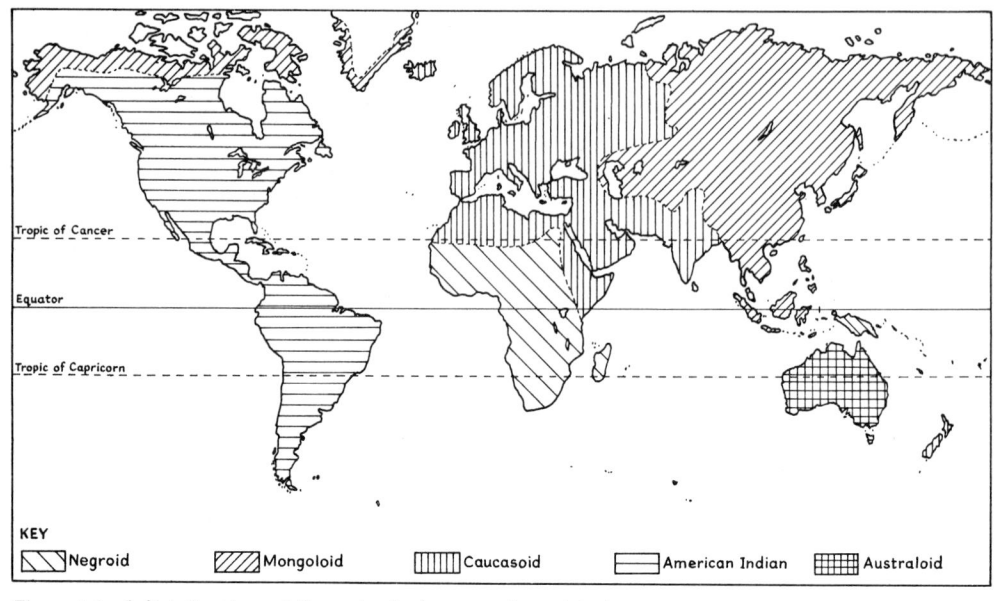

KEY: Negroid | Mongoloid | Caucasoid | American Indian | Australoid

The original distribution of the principal races of mankind

were only people one heard strange tales about and rarely, if ever, met. Today, we not only meet them, but have to live and work with people of different races, and whether we can all live together in peace is not yet known.

Liberty and equality are the big problems. Up to quite recent times, the white people seemed to be having the best of everything. They spread into many parts of the world and used their superior power to colonise, to build great empires and to rule millions of subject people. Then the two world wars in the first half of this century helped to destroy this power. As a result, though the white people still remain rich, most of the people they once ruled are now ruling themselves.

In fact, a world-wide revolution is taking place. Subject people everywhere are claiming equality with those who once ruled them. They will not be satisfied until there are no more subject people or second-class citizens in the world.

1. In your school, are there children of other races beside your own? Which races are they? What do you know about life in those parts of the world from which they come?
2. What did Paul mean by his words at the head of this chapter that all men are of one blood? Do any of the other quotations seem to agree with him? Do you also agree?

A white girl in Cicero, Chicago, carries a skunk to symbolize her attitude to the Negroes wishing to integrate her district.

[30] RACE

No more subject races! There are still many places in the world where this is not true. Two of them which have serious racial problems are the U.S.A. and South Africa.

America

A small group of negro leaders were chatting on the balcony of the Lorraine Motel in Memphis. It was Thursday evening April 4, 1968. Suddenly, a shot rang out and one of them collapsed fatally wounded. He was Dr. Martin Luther King, aged 39, who had been the leader of the American negroes in their struggle for freedom and equality. His death was followed by the worst race riots that America has ever known.

The four million negro slaves in America were freed by Abraham Lincoln in 1863. For a hundred years most of their descendants have existed, ill-housed, ill-educated, ill-paid, frightened and bewildered in a country growing steadily richer and more powerful.

Today there are nineteen million of them. Until recently they earned on average under half what a white man received for similar work. They have been the first to suffer from unemployment, for it is only recently that American trade unions have begun to give up their colour bar. In the northern cities many of them live in black ghettos, overcrowded and insanitary. In the south, laws which have been passed to give them fairer treatment, as for example in education, are often ignored.

But in recent years the mood of the negroes has changed. Dr. King expressed their determination to win equality with white people. 'We want all our rights and we want them *here* and we want them *now*,' he declared. And in thirteen years he was able to win for them many concessions: the right to share travel, lunch counters, libraries and parks with white people.

Like Gandhi he believed in non-violence. 'If you will protest courageously and yet with dignity and Christian love, when the history books are written in future generations, the historians will have to pause and say, 'There lived a great people a black people — who injected new meaning and new dignity into the veins of civilisation'.'

Not everyone agreed with Dr. King. It is hard to see police dogs set on negro children, bombs thrown into crowded negro Sunday Schools, defenceless demonstrators clubbed and beaten with iron bars without feeling the urge to retaliate.

'If America don't come round, we've got to burn America down,' declared H. Rap Brown, a Black Power leader. Black Power intended to fight for freedom, and at a conference in Newark in 1967 demanded a division of America into black and white countries or, in other words, a negro republic inside the United States. Black Power has declined since then, which is fortunate because it could have led to much bloodshed. But advance is being made slowly in other ways. The Rev. Jesse Jackson, one of the principal black leaders, feels the best policy should be a non-militant one: the black community everywhere should insist on their rights and take their full place in society.

South Africa

The population of South Africa consists of just over four million whites and twenty million non-whites. The non-whites consist of Africans, Asians and Coloureds (mixed blood). Of these twenty million, eighteen and a half million are Africans. The white population is a mixture of people of British and Dutch origin. The Dutch are the more numerous and are known as Africaners; their language is Africaans.

The non-whites have always been regarded as inferiors and are firmly controlled by the white inhabitants. Each of them, for instance, is required to carry a pass-book which records personal details and states the area in which the owner is allowed to live. Failure to produce one's pass-book on demand can result in arrest and detention. One is not allowed outside one's living area nor to move house nor to change one's job without permission.

Large numbers of men, however, in order to provide the essentials of life for their families, are forced to leave their homes and work in industrial areas which can be hundreds of miles away. They are housed in huge hostels furnished with bunk beds in crowded dormitories. Their pay is generally only a fraction of white pay for similar work. They are allowed to return to their families for only one month in each year.

Partly to overcome these inhuman conditions, some wives and families have tried moving to waste ground near the cities and have built for themselves corrugated iron shacks. These shanty towns are illegal and every so often the authorities have bull-dozed them at short notice. Sometimes at two or three in the morning.

Black children, compared with white children, have very little spent on their education. The law requires that they be taught in Africaans which, of course, is not their native language and is of little use to them. This was one of the reasons for the protest organised in Soweto in 1976 when many children were killed and wounded by the police who are quite ruthless in stamping out opposition to the regime. Later, as adolescents, they have small chance of attending the country's universities which were built mainly by black labour.

Black Power salute from a policeman in Philadelphia

South African negroes, unlike those in America, have no vote in national elections and cannot own freehold property. The formation of unions to protect their working interests has been strongly discouraged.

In recent years the South African government has introduced a policy of "Homelands", by which it has set aside certain areas of land where Africans can live in independence. But as they are completely surrounded by white South Africa the independence must be far from complete. Moreover, the size of these areas is small compared with the rest of the country and with the large population they are expected to cater for.

Young people of this generation are very concerned about justice and no doubt you feel indignant that anyone in the world can be treated in this way. These tragic conditions must be altered, and it is certainly true that if the white man does not alter them, the black people one day surely will, and not by peaceful means.

In these circumstances what can anyone do? Processions and demonstrations of protest are popular nowadays. They are one way of 'letting off steam' but they don't achieve very much, because they do not offer any practical solution.

Indignation is not enough. On more than one occasion Jesus made it clear that Christians should use their brains as well as their emotions. "Be as wise as serpents," he said. And men like Martin Luther King were successful because of their wise and thoughtful campaigning to improve conditions.

We must not be one-sided in our judgments. In America, for instance, most white young people are no more responsible for the race problem than we are. It arose from events that took place centuries ago and for which other countries including Britain were partly responsible. This is also true of South Africa.

There are many people in the United States and in South Africa working for better conditions. We might do well to study what they are doing and saying about them. The solution is not an easy one.

Britain also has a race problem. It is estimated that by 1985 the number of the non-white people in Britain will have grown to two and a half million. The difficulties that these people have in settling in a 'white' country are reflected in two serious Acts that the British Parliament has passed: The Commonwealth Immigrants Act of 1962 and the Race Relations Act of 1968.

'Foreign Affairs' when your parents were young meant chiefly keeping the peace between nations. Now an even tougher problem has been added to it: keeping the peace between races. It is a new problem and in discussing it beware of ignorance and prejudice. Begin yourself, if you can, with an open mind and, if you want a point of view, read again what the great religions have to say at

Dr Martin Luther King

the beginning of this chapter and remember the words of Martin Luther King,
> *We must all learn to live together like brothers or we shall all perish together like fools.*

Passages from the Bible for further study.

Matthew 23, 8–11	All brothers
Galations 3, 20–28	All sons of God
Acts 10, 34–35	God accepts all nations
Matthew 5, 9	Peacemakers
Romans 12, 10–21	Love one another

For Discussion

On this subject, background knowledge is essential.
Organised group research in class would be very helpful.

1. Find out all you can about the two acts of Parliament mentioned in this chapter. Are there any provisions in these Acts with which you disagree? Can you think of any other regulations that should be made?
2. Study a map of the West Indies. Find out what life is like out there and then discuss the big differences immigrants from the West Indies will find when they settle in this country. If you know boys and girls who have come from the West Indies, persuade them, if you can, to give a talk to your class on this subject.
3. The study in question 2 could well be repeated in reference to immigrants from other countries, Pakistan and India, for example.
4. Write down *three* ways in which ordinary people can help to foster good relations between different races in this country. If you have immigrants in your class, their point of view will be important in discussing this question.
5. Are there any race problems in the area in which you live? How do you think they should be solved?
6. White people in South Africa feel that their problems are not understood by the people in Britain. It is all too easy, they think, for people 5000 miles away to pronounce judgement upon them; they do not have to face the situation themselves. In all fairness then, you should get someone who has lived in South Africa to speak to you on race problems and to answer your

A famous African doctor with his wife and children

questions. Failing this, learn all you can about South Africa. Apart from encyclopaedias and other books in your library, information can be obtained from South Africa House, Institute of Race Relations (247 Pentonville Road, London N1), Christian Action (Amen Court, London EC4), Commission for Racial Equality (Eliot House, Allington Street, London SW1) and short films from Concord Films Council (Ipswich, Suffolk). Find out

a: when colonists first arrived in South Africa and where they came from
b: what conditions were like when the first settlers arrived.
c: how they developed the country.
d: how the race problem gradually arose.
e: what the 'whites' have done for the native population.

With this information, you could arrange a good debate, especially if two or three of you took the part of South African school children whose families had been settled there for several generations.

7. 'I wouldn't marry an English girl because it would not be fair to take her back to my own country where life for women is very different.' What are the problems of inter-racial marriage? Would you welcome a 'mixed marriage' in your family? Why? In what circumstances would it be wise?

8. How would you reply to this type of comment?
    a: 'They're not civilised like us!'
    b: 'They come here and take our jobs.'
    c: 'A white man shouldn't have to take orders from a black boss.'
    d: 'Foreigners should stay in their own country.'

Work

*He who does not help to turn the rolling wheels
of this great world lives a lost life.*   Hindu saying

Say not, I am a great man and work is below my dignity.
Jewish saying (The Talmud)

If anyone does not work, neither should he eat.   Paul

God is gracious to him who earns his living by his own labour.   Mohammed

*He who performs diligently and contentedly the work allotted to him,
whatever it may be, lays hold of perfection.*   Hindu saying

Never choose an occupation that is considered bad.   Buddhist scriptures

Give the labourer his wages before his perspiration is dry.   Mohammed

Whatever you do, do it to the glory of God.   Paul

'I'm only here for the money!' Unfortunately there are millions of people who can say that quite truthfully about their daily work.

We live in a machine age, and the more machines we have, the more man becomes a machine himself. His work becomes mechanical and boring and apart from the people he meets and the friends he makes, very little else attracts him about the job he does. An industrial chaplain who has spent many years working in different factories takes a very serious view of this. 'Modern machinery,' he says, 'is destroying men.'

For such people there is some hope in the future. As mentioned in the chapter on Leisure, with the advance of automation the number of hours we have to work each day should be reduced. 'The best we can hope for,' said Bertrand Russell, 'is to diminish the hours of work. Four hours' boredom is a thing most people could endure without damage.'

Of course, there are ways of avoiding the dull, mechanical jobs, if you have the will and the ability to do so. One is — as you have no doubt been told many times — to get the highest qualifications you can while you are still at school. Another is to accept lower wages for a year or two in order to learn a trade or **profession. This is especially important during periods of high employment.**

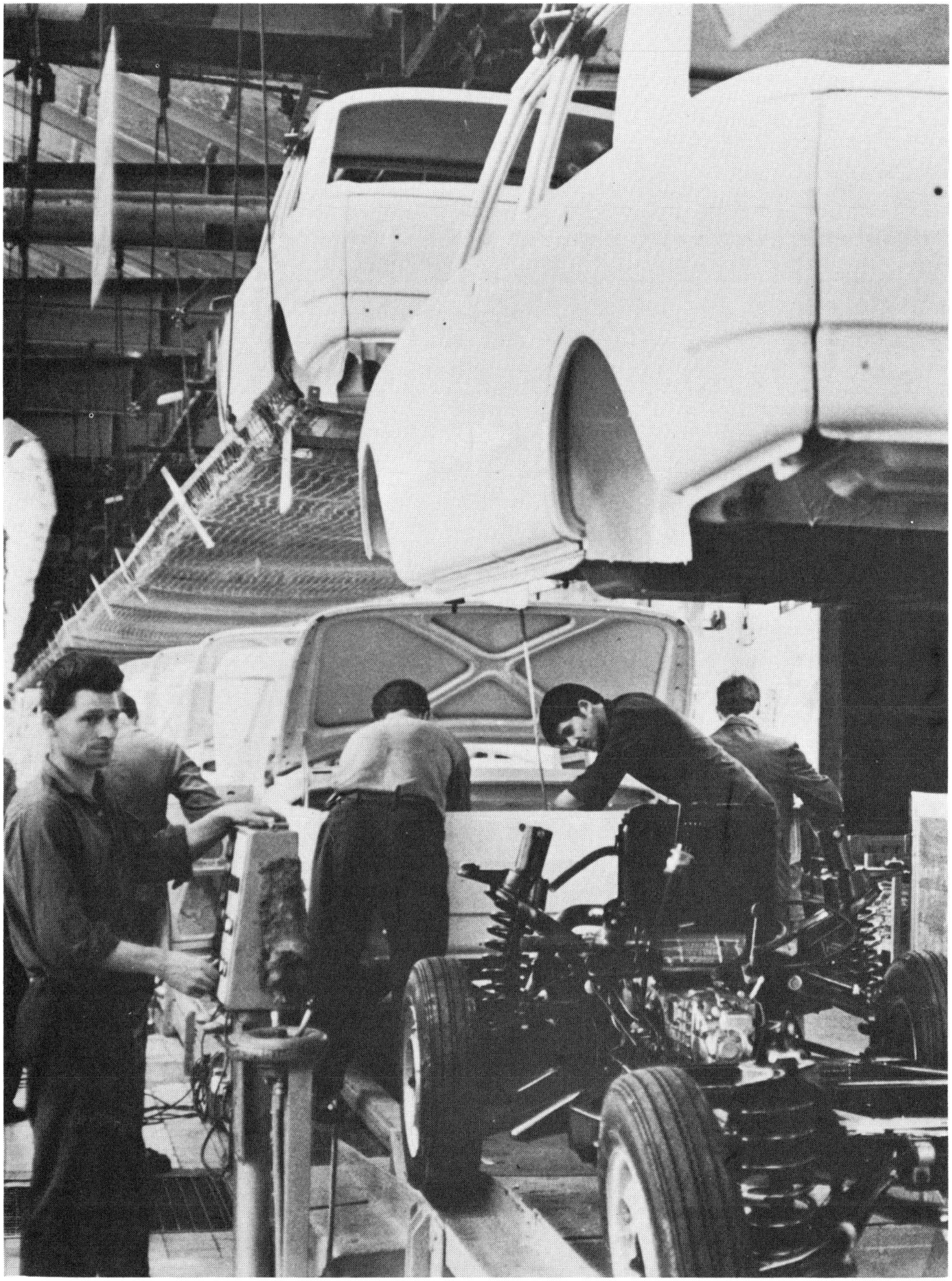

[40] WORK

Don't be 'wise after the event'! A factory doctor made a survey of nearly 2000 teenagers between 15 and 18 years of age. He reports meeting a considerable number who said the same thing: how sorry they were that their parents had not insisted on that extra year at school or on the apprenticeship that was open to them when they left. Parents who tend to say, 'Please yourself' are not always being kind.

Lest you think this argument is just another case of 'being got at,' take a look at the medical evidence.

Dr. Peter Taylor, an acknowledged expert on absenteeism in industry made a detailed study of the subject. He says, 'What we do find is that absenteeism is highest in people who lack job satisfaction . . . The illnesses brought on by such problems of 'job dissatisfaction' are real enough. Nervous anxiety produces real backaches, real headaches, real peptic ulcers, real heart ailments. People who get an illness in this way have even been known to die of it.'

This is why you should take great care in choosing and preparing for your job. It is an important decision you have to make at the wrong end of life, when you still know next to nothing about the work-a-day world. Listen to everybody with experience of it. Many things they have learnt can help you in your choice. In addition, there are books on careers in the library and the Department of Education and Science issue pamphlets giving information on a great number of jobs.

The lucky people, perhaps, are those that know well beforehand exactly what they want to do with their lives. Some of them have what is called 'a sense of vocation.'

'Vocation' comes from a Latin word meaning 'to call.' A vocation is a calling and has usually to do with religion. People feel called by God to give some service to the community. Money and hours of work don't matter as much as the work itself.

Christianity, in particular, has had this effect on men and women in every generation. Many of the greatest reforms have been brought about by such people. For many years, for example, not a single hospital or school existed among the very poor nations except those built and staffed by Christian pioneers.

In Matthew 25 Christ speaks about the need to help the hungry, the lonely, the ill-clothed, the sick and the prisoner. 'Anything you do,' he says, 'for one of these my brothers, however, humble, you do it for me.'

But one does not need to be religious to have a vocation. 'Mr. F. has left us,' the estate agent told me one day. 'He has gone to take up work helping people discharged from prison. He has wanted to do it for a long time. He's given up a very good salary.' Many people, like Mr. F., just feel that the world is in a bad state and that there is something that they could be good at doing which would help to make things better.

In one sense, almost any job can be looked upon in this way, for when we do something really well we are giving satisfaction not only to ourselves but also to those we do it for. Every day, people suffer inconvenience, annoyance, and sometimes sheer misery from work badly and inefficiently done. A good workman benefits everyone.

This is particularly true for Christians. Dr. Wilfred Grenfell, who spent his life in helping the Eskimos in Labrador, said, 'Following Christ is doing something, anything well.'

1: Read the Hindu saying at the beginning of this chapter. Do you agree with it? Give your reasons.
2: Write down a list of all the jobs that you think can be specially called vocations. What makes them so?

Before you leave school you reach the fifth or sixth form. Probably you win prizes, do well in sport or some other activity. You may even become a prefect! In any case, as a senior pupil you are important and count for something.

Then the time comes to leave and start work and suddenly your position is reversed. You are once again a junior among older people. The hours are long, the work at first rather trivial and boring and you don't lord it over anybody any more.

At first you may be overwhelmed by the adult world in which you find yourself. Then gradually the shyness wears off and you feel accepted. You begin almost unconsciously to copy the dress, speech and manners of those about you.

In this desire to conform you may come up against another problem. You discover that the usual standards of behaviour accepted in school and at home are challenged. You meet people who, so far as their job is concerned, ridicule honesty and truthfulness. Whilst they would never steal from you, they will steal quite cheerfully from the firm. 'Everybody does it!' they declare, whether it refers to petty pilfering or lying about the work they do.

What are you to do? You can't say very much and you can't alter things. It is really a question of whether you have the moral courage to stick to your own principles (where possible) and risk being laughed at.

It will be strange if you can go through your life without your moral courage being challenged at all. Sometimes the decision is not easy to make. Take this for example:

[42] WORK

What are you going to do, Jim?

I'm going in to work on Monday. What else?

You're not! You won't be popular, you know.

I can't help that. I didn't vote for the strike, did I? This is a free country, isn't it? I don't think it's right to stay out. I've got to do what I think's right, haven't I?

You've got to think about the wife and kids, Jim. They could suffer as well as you.

Oh, I'm sick of this place! There's never any peace. Half the disputes are just plain stupid. And look at the unemployed. Aren't there enough of them? If we go on like this we'll all be out of a job soon.

Jim is obviously worried. He has a loyalty to his conscience, his family, his mates and his firm.

1: What is the easiest thing for Jim to do?
2: What advice would you give him in these circumstances?
3: Suppose everybody similarly placed took your advice, would that be a good thing? Why?

Working conditions will no doubt alter a great deal during your lifetime.

For example, you have heard of 'Women's Lib.' (Women's Liberation Movement)? This movement wants complete equality between the sexes especially in regard to work and the home.

Years ago it was generally acknowledged that 'a woman's place is in the home.' Many married women are quite satisfied with this role and want nothing else. But increasing numbers of them now go out to work. They prefer an outside occupation and, of course, it helps to swell the family income.

But what happens when children come? The woman has to give up her job and, if there are a number of children, she is tied to the home for some years.

Women's Lib. argues that a woman trained for her job is as important as a man (certainly, the country could not run without women working). She should therefore be able to keep her job. But what about the family? Is the answer the day nursery everywhere, as in Russia? (We discuss this under 'Family.') Or should the husband and wife share in running the home, working possibly alternate weeks?

It is an interesting problem. What do you think about it?

WORK [43]

Passages from the Bible for further study

Matt. 25, 14–29	What God expects of us
Matt. 25, 31–45	A Christian's duty
Luke 12, 13–21	Working for the wrong reasons
Col. 3, 23,24	A Christian's reasons for work

[44] WORK

Acts 18, 1–4 } Paul works for a living
II Thess. 3, 7–12 }

Proverbs 6, 6–11   The penalties of idleness.
                    (No welfare state!)

Proverbs 26, 13–16 The slothful man

For Discussion

1. What is the difference between having a lot to live on and having a lot to live for? Give examples, if you can of both. If you had to choose one or the other, which would you go for?
2. Bishop Huddleston, who spent many years working among Africans in South Africa, said that one of the main differences between the African and the Englishman was the Englishman's need for security. The African lives for today; the Englishman, for tomorrow. Why do you think this is so? What effect does it have on your choice of a job?
3. Why do all the quotations at the head of this chapter stress the need to work whether you are rich or poor?
4. Comment on the following:
   a: Those who work hardest grumble least.
   b: No-one works unless he is paid for it.
   c: Everybody does a little bit of fiddling when he can.
   d: You can't be in business and remain a Christian.
5. In school what subjects do you like best? Why do you like them? Does this help you in thinking about what you would like to do when you leave?
6. Make a list of
   a: poor reasons
   b: good reasons for choosing a job.
7. Write down three jobs you could be seriously interested in. Find out all you can about them (Careers teacher, school library, Youth Employment Service, Department of Education and Science). Write down against each
   a: Why you are attracted to the job
   b: The qualifications needed
   c: The starting wages
   d: The prospects (promotion, etc.)

WORK [45]

8. Find out all you can about the Tolpuddle Martyrs and write a short essay on Trade Unions.
9. In a recent survey of young people at work, the following statement was made: 'Young people from homes with a religious background showed a noticeable sense of responsibility.' Why do you think this is so?

War and violence

Weapons of war are tools of evil;
those who truly admire them are murderers at heart.   Tao saying

Where troops march, there will thorns spring up;
and where armies are gathered, there famine will enter.   Tao saying

Never steal, never kill, and never do anything
you may later regret or be ashamed of.   Buddha

Fight in the way of Allah with those who fight you, but you do not begin the
hostilities; for Allah does not love aggressors.   Mohammed

They shall beat their swords into ploughshares, and their spears into pruning
hooks; nation shall not lift up sword against nation, neither shall they learn war
any more.   Isaiah

As much as lies within your power, live peaceably with all men.   Paul

Blessed are the peacemakers, for they shall be called the children of God.   Jesus

World War I ended at the eleventh hour of the eleventh day of the eleventh month of 1918. It had meant nothing, solved nothing, and proved nothing; and in so doing had killed 8,538,315 men and seriously wounded 21,219,452. Of 7,750,919 others taken prisoner or missing, well over a million were later presumed dead; thus the total deaths (not counting civilians) approached ten million.

One of the war leaders (Woodrow Wilson) later admitted that the war had been fought for business interests; another (David Lloyd George) had told a newspaperman, 'If people really knew, the war would be stopped tomorrow, but of course they don't — and can't know. The correspondents don't write and the censorship wouldn't pass the truth. The thing is horrible, and beyond human nature to bear, and I feel I cannot go on any longer with the bloody business. . . . '.' (In Flanders Fields by Leon Wolff)

World War II is nearer our time. It cannot be said that it solved no problem, for it overthrew a terrible tyranny — Nazism. But the cost again was tremendous, mainly in terms of civilian lives in crowded cities, concentration camps and as refugees fleeing from their ruined homes. For example, on February 14 and 15,

WAR AND VIOLENCE [47]

1945, 135,000 people were killed in British and American air attacks on one city alone, Dresden (twice as many as died from the atom bomb on Hiroshima). Afterwards it was admitted that the attack on Dresden was really unnecessary to the winning of the war.

What of future wars? Bombs can now be used that are 500 times more powerful than the Hiroshima bomb which killed 70,000 people. President Kennedy was saying as far back as 1963 that 'a full scale nuclear exchange, lasting less than sixty minutes could wipe out more than 300 million Americans, Europeans and Russians, as well as untold numbers elsewhere.' Today, the devastation would be much greater even than this and what the late Russian leader, Kruschev, told the Chinese is all the more true now. 'Those that survived a nuclear war,' he said, 'would envy the dead.'

So the nuclear war of the future will mean race suicide. Despite this obvious fact, the Great Powers still manufacture nuclear weapons and invent elaborate warning systems which will enable them to let loose this mass destruction at a few minutes' notice. The old Balance of Power in the world has now been replaced by the Balance of Terror.

Think too of the 'small wars' that have taken place in the world during the last few years. None of these could have happened if the Great Powers had not permitted the manufacture and sale of armaments. This is a very profitable business and it is estimated that more than thirty million people in the world are engaged on the making and distributing of arms.

The cost to mankind, too, is enormous. Britain, for example, spends about £2.82 per week per head of the population on Defence compared with £3.33 on Education and 27p on helping under-developed countries.

This problem of war is linked with two other problems we have considered, race and poverty. There is no doubt that world disaster awaits us all unless more and more people in every country join forces to solve them. World rulers eventually would pay attention to the growing and insistent demands of those they rule.

1: Look at the first Tao saying at the beginning of this chapter. Do you agree with it?
2: How are the problems of race and world poverty linked with war and violence?

The violence of war may seem a long way off, but what about the violence of peace? This is on our door-step. Here, for example, are some random items of news:
"Nineteen policemen were injured last night as they battled with a rampaging mob of youths. The rioters swept through the streets of

Hiroshima 1945

RSPCA 1971 (with help from local Fire Brigade)

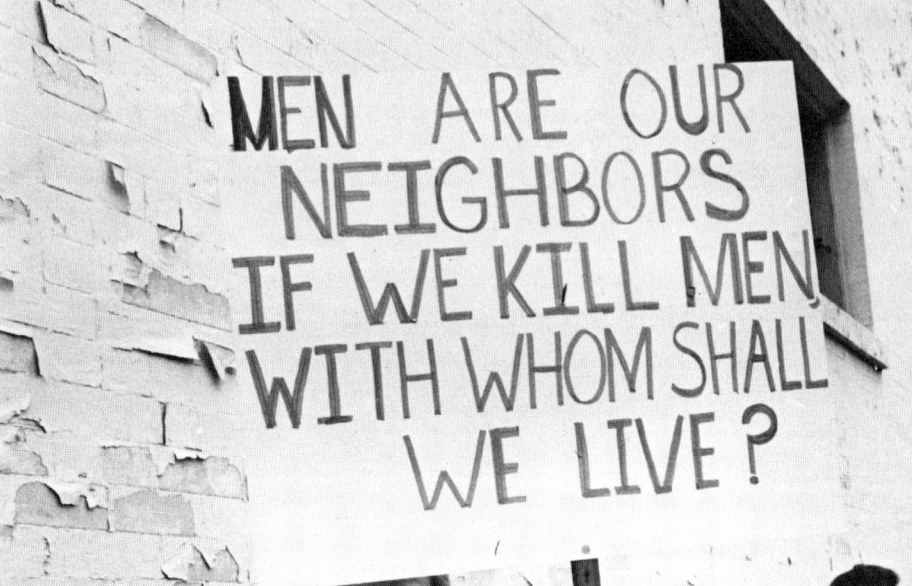

MEN ARE OUR NEIGHBORS IF WE KILL MEN, WITH WHOM SHALL WE LIVE?

WAR AND VIOLENCE [51]

Bristol looting shops and setting fire to cars and buildings.
After six hours of clashes the police pulled out of the city's battered St. Paul's area".

"Police fired tear gas to break up rioting of British soccer fans during England's opening European championship match against Belgium in Turin. About 100 British fans charged across the partially filled terraces and dozens of fights broke out. Six spectators were taken to hospital, one with serious head injuries".

"Horrific week-end riots broke out in Miami after three policemen were cleared of beating a black man to death. The violence left nineteen dead, most of them whites, savagely massacred by gangs of enraged blacks. Later frenzied car loads of "White avengers" roared through the streets opening fire at random on black pedestrians".

Crimes of violence have increased rapidly over the last ten years. In many cities there are areas now where ordinary citizens cannot walk about at night in safety. Much of this violence is the work of young people moving about in gangs and in many cases there is no sense or reason behind it. People are injured, sometimes killed, as a group of young men admitted recently, just 'for the fun of it.'

More serious still is the official sanction given to violence. In many countries it is commonplace for the police to use great brutality against demonstrators and to 'beat-up' those whom they arrest. Governments permit and appear to encourage the torture and persecution of those that oppose them.

In 1948 the United Nations issued 'A Universal Declaration of Human Rights.' In it they declared that men are born free and equal in rights and dignity. Everyone should enjoy freedom of thought, conscience, speech and religion and should have equal protection before the law. For millions, today, this declaration must seem to be a mockery.

What do world religions teach about this problem?

Buddhism is pacifist. The quotation from Buddha at the head of this chapter emphasises this. Apart from Japanese Buddhism, Buddhists have generally set an excellent example to the world of living at peace and not resorting to war. They are so concerned about war in the west that they send missionaries to Europe to convert us to Buddhism.

Mohammed sanctioned war, in particular where it was in defence of his teaching. He was, in fact, a great warrior himself. 'The Holy War' was common in the early days, when his religion was spreading rapidly. Today, the Arab world will fight to defend land and property and do so in the name of Allah.

The Jews in their early history fought for land and in defence of it. They did so

WAR AND VIOLENCE

feeling the blessing of God was upon them. This is true today when they fight in defence of Israel.

The greatest puzzle, you may think, is Christianity.

'Do not set yourself against the man who wrongs you. If someone slaps you on the right cheek, turn and offer him your left. If a man in authority makes you go one mile, go with him two.'

'Love your enemies and pray for your persecutors .... If you do not forgive others then the wrongs you have done will not be forgiven by your Father.'

Surely these words of Jesus are as pacifist as any words of Buddha! Yet the two great wars of this century were fought mainly between Christian countries. The history of Christian civilisation is one of recurring wars, some even begun by the Christian church. A Christian priest is not allowed to take up arms but he may bless the members of his congregation when they go to war.

Is this a denial of the teaching of Jesus? Many Christians think so. Amongst them are the Quakers, who in time of war are conscientious objectors. That is, they will take any action to help the victims on either side – and many have shown great bravery in this – but they will not fight.

The majority of Christians, however, seem to think that the spread of tyranny, such as Hitler's, should be stopped at all costs, and that Christ would approve of fighting to defend one's homeland from it. They also believe it is a Christian duty to stop the violent criminal by any means necessary.

On both sides of this argument you have thoughtful views held by very sincere people. It would be foolish to accuse either side of hypocrisy.

What do you think is the teaching of Jesus on this subject, and how should it be applied today? First you should read for yourself the teaching and example of Jesus as given to us in the passages for study below.

Passages from the Bible for further study

Matt. 5, 38–48	Loving your enemies
Matt. 26, 52	Jesus and the sword
Luke 9, 51–56	Jesus rebukes James and John
Luke 23, 32–34	Jesus forgives his enemies
Matt. 10, 28	Those who kill the body
Romans 13, 1–10	Obeying the government
Colossians 3, 12–17	Forgiving and loving one another
Ephesians 6, 10–17	The armour of God

An eight metre figure of Christ, made out of the metal of Argentinian guns, erected in 1904 3500 metres above sea level on the boundary of Argentina and Chile. On the granite plinth these words are inscribed: 'Sooner shall these mountains crumble into dust than shall Argentinians and Chileans break the peace which, at the feet of Christ the Redeemer, they have sworn to maintain.'

[54] WAR AND VIOLENCE

For Discussion

1. 'We act with ruthlessness like a steamroller – bombing extensive areas, and not selected targets based on detailed intelligence' General Johnson, U.S. Chief of Staff – the Vietnam War.

    Do you consider that the use of force
    a: by a nation or
    b: by an individual is ever justified? If your answer to (a) is no, what are the effective alternatives?
2. 'Don't let it happen; do something now!' we are told. How do you think nuclear war can be avoided? What can ordinary people do to prevent its taking place? You should consider here the possible causes of future wars.
3. Find out and discuss our own country's policy in regard to nuclear weapons.
4. Write to the United Nations Association (address p. 16) for information about how it is constituted and how it works.
5. Find out why the U.N. failed in its early years and how it has recovered some of its authority. How can it be made more effective in solving world problems?
6. Find out what you can about the International Court of Justice. Why is it not being used today to settle the most serious international disputes?
7. A famous British judge, Lord Justice Birkett, said that he considered that no violence should be shown on television. Do you agree? Give your reasons.
8. What makes young people act violently? What can be done about it?
9. Keep the copies of your daily newspaper for one week. Then list briefly all the acts of violence reported in them. The different kinds of violence in your lists could then be discussed in class and also the means that ordinary citizens could take to reduce them.
10. How can
    a: the police
    b: magistrates and judges
    c: the government help to reduce crimes of violence?

Leisure

He who sees how action may be rest and rest action — he is wisest among his kind; he has the truth. He does well acting or resting. Hindu saying.

Be still and know that I am God. Psalms.

If you take no liberties, your liberties will not be curtailed. Confucianist saying.

With coarse food to eat, water to drink, and a bent arm for a pillow, happiness may still be found. Confucius.

'What are you going to do with your spare time?' This question may soon become as important for the Careers teacher to ask as 'What job do you want to do?'

Just over a century ago a small boy gave this account of himself to a Commission of Enquiry:

> I am thirteen. I do not know how long I have worked. I wedge clay for a thrower. I come at 6 o'clock . . . I sometimes give over at 6.30 at night, sometimes at 7 and 8. I get 4/6 a week. I can't read. I go to school sometimes on Sundays.

There was not much leisure for him, nor even for people at the beginning of this century when hours of work were very long. In fact, some people worked nearly all their waking hours just to provide food and shelter for themselves and their children.

Today we are better off. Only half our waking hours are normally spent at work and we get two or three or even four weeks' paid holiday a year.

The future is going to be even brighter. By the end of the 1980's, we are told, most people will not even start work till their mid-twenties and will retire in their mid-fifties. During their working life they will have about three leisure days per week. By means of the silicon chip, this could very well happen if it were utilised for the benefit of everyone.

But will it be brighter? Leisure, like money, can be a great deceiver. The more we have of it, we imagine, the happier we shall be. This, in your case, could be quite untrue. 'Work never did anyone any harm,' it is sometimes said. But leisure can be disastrous.

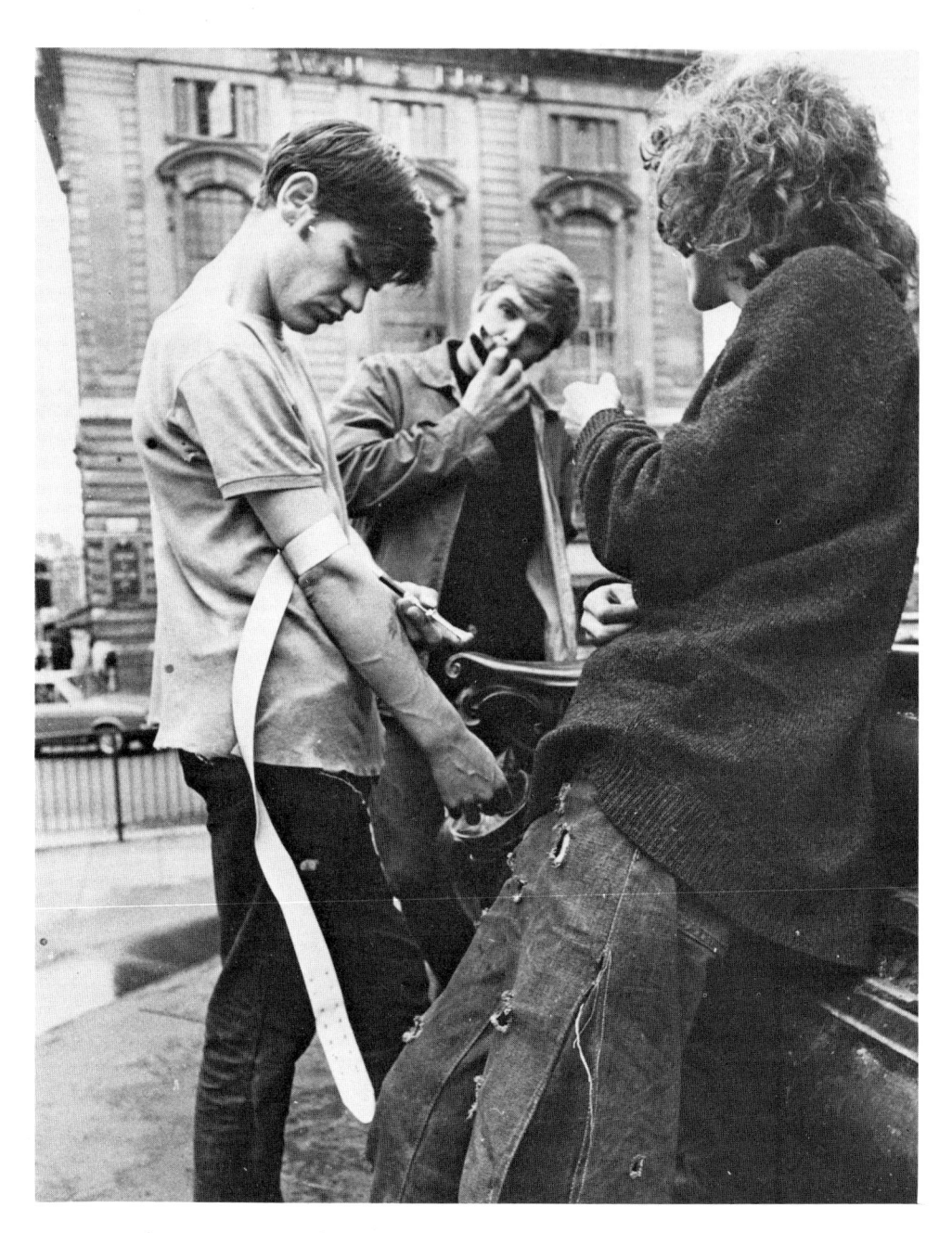

Junkies in Piccadilly Circus

LEISURE [57]

Time 7 p.m. Any evening of the week.
David and Terry are propping up a wall at the end of the street. John appears across the road.

David	Hi John! Where are you off to?
John	Nowhere. (He crosses the road) What's on tonight?
Terry	Don't know. You say.
John	What about the Club then?
David	Closed. Old Bowdler's on holiday.
John	Let's go to the caff.
Terry	No money.
John	You don't need any. We just sit near the door and scarper when . . .
Terry	Do we? Ha! Ha! Ha! You tell that to my Dad. I shall get half killed if I get into trouble again.
	(A long silence)
David	Oh, come on, I'm bored. Let's do something *quick*.
John	Hey, boys! See what I see?
David	What?
John	Over there — those two!
Terry	Two of the Anselm mob, ain't it?
John	Come on, quick! Let's kick 'em in!

What happens then may well end up in hospital and/or the police station. Cause? Surplus energy without outlet. Result? Boredom. And boredom breeds trouble.

Every year over a million pounds worth of damage is done to trains, railway track and fencing. Stone throwing injures crews and passengers, signals and telegraph apparatus are damaged, hundreds of carriages ripped up. And we, the general public, meekly pay for it all. But some things can never be paid for. A stone dropped from a bridge killed a train driver recently.

At the time of writing two small girls have died, falling over the edge of a cliff. Someone with nothing better to do smashed the fence guarding the danger area.

Hooliganism, much of it unreported, accounts for damage and suffering on a wide scale and is mainly the result of boredom. So of course are drug taking and alcoholism, both of which are seriously on the increase.

Older people, too, suffer from boredom. Television becomes a nightly drug (turn it on when you come in from work; turn it off at bedtime). The remarkable spread of Bingo and other forms of gambling accounts for eight thousand million pounds worth of spending in Britain every year.

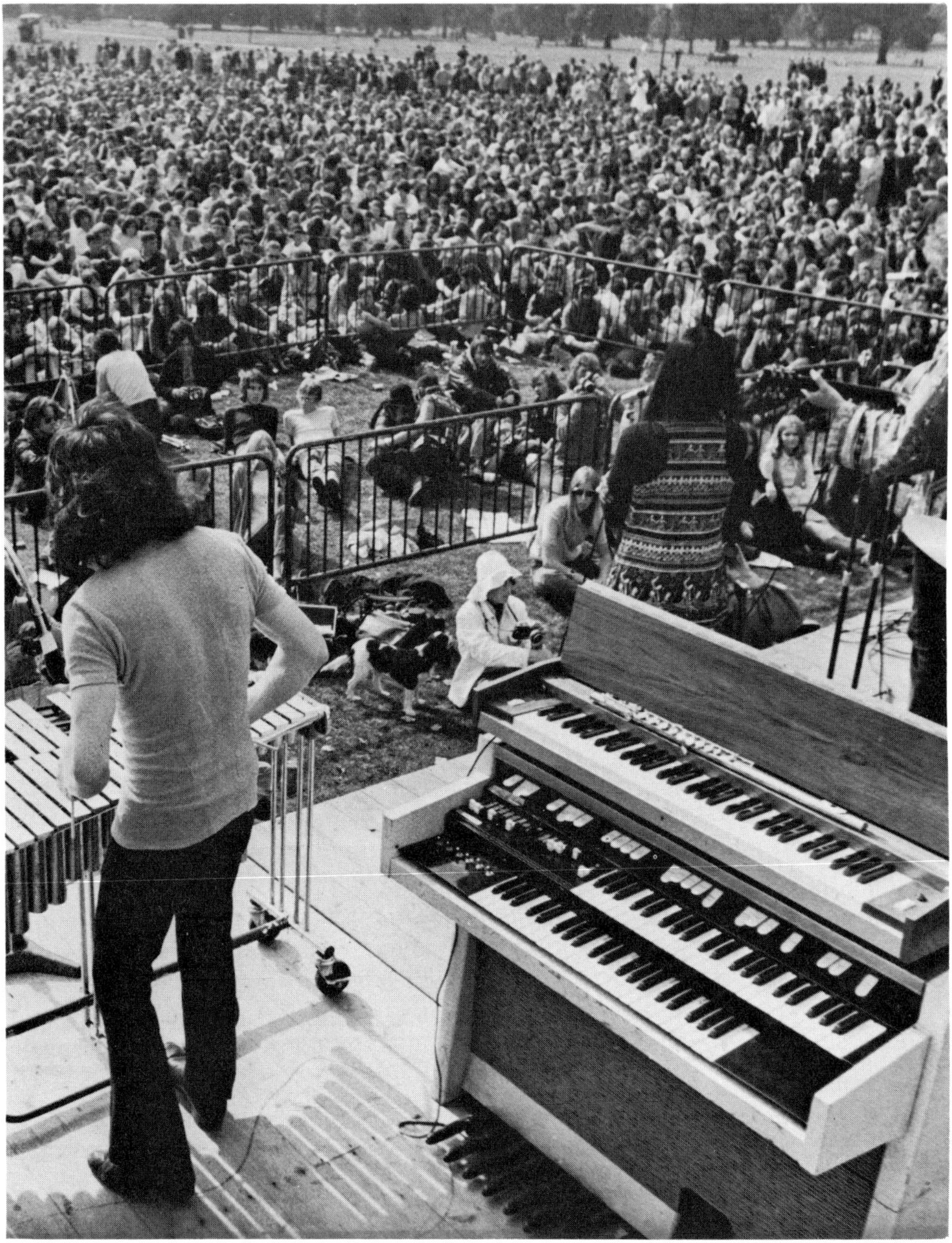

LEISURE [59]

Yet we live in a marvellous world and a wonderful age. Science has opened up for us activities and interests never known before in the history of man. 'I shall be away for a fortnight,' said my window-cleaner the other day. 'I'm going to Algiers for my holiday.' Fifty years ago it is doubtful if a window-cleaner could have afforded the time and money to go to Southend or Blackpool for a weekend.

1: When during the day or the week do you find yourself getting bored?
2: What can you do to prevent it?
3: *Drinking on the Increase*
Over 100,000 arrests for drunkeness are taken annually through the courts. In 1978, according to the Chief Constable's report, there were 108,000 proved offences compared with 99,274 five years previously. A report on "Alcohol and Work" stresses that teenagers can slip into alcoholism and have problems much more quickly than older people.

Why is this so, do you think?
What reasons, other than boredom, account for people drinking too much?
Why in the last five years is there an increase in offenders?

You may be among the lucky ones who have no problems in filling in their leisure time or you may be among the many that moan because, for example, 'There isn't a decent club round here. There's nothing to do at night. Everything's dead!'

There may be good reason for your complaint, but it is little use moaning about it. In any case, the world isn't going to devote itself to making you happy. You will have to do it for yourself. Think about your leisure time sensibly and do some planning for it, especially in school holidays. There is nothing so exhausting as doing nothing. 'The best definition of hell,' said Bernard Shaw, 'is a perpetual holiday.'

Look at the word 'recreation.' Your spare time should help you to re-create your mind and body after a day's or a week's work. If it does just that, you will get some real satisfaction from it.

But what are you to do? Work carefully through the questions at the end of this chapter. If there is nothing at all that appeals to you, it will be a judgement on your character, rather than on the world in which you are living.

Religious people do not have difficulty with this problem. This may seem

[60] LEISURE

surprising, since there are so few quotations at the head of this chapter. But Christianity, for example, is a way of life, and Christ's teaching governs both leisure and work. A large group of young people connected with a local church have the following regular activities:

    helping the physically handicapped
    visiting a Children's Home
    decorating
    playgroups
    reading to the blind
    helping at a men's care unit
    holiday work camps
    scouts and guides
    work with old people and in youth clubs
    Amnesty International
    tape-recording hospital messages
    singing to down and outs
    hobbies club for children
    visiting prisoners and hospital patients

Many young people today, Christian or otherwise, show themselves keen to help other people in need, if they can find a means of doing it. Some of these activities are suitable for your age group. There are many others, and an organisation like Task Force would put you in touch with them.

Passages from the Bible for further study

Matt. 25, 31–46	active leisure
Luke 10, 25–42	service and meditation
Mark 6, 30–32	prayer and meditation
Romans 12	Christian brotherliness

By map and compass: a six days' trek in pursuit of a Duke of Edinburgh's Scheme Gold Award

Task Force at work

LEISURE [63]

For Discussion

1. The Opinion Research Centre made a special investigation into spare time activities in Britain. (The results were reported in the London *Evening Standard*.) People were asked to say *to which two activities* they gave most spare time and the following details emerged:

	I Most enjoy doing		II Most time given	
	Men	Women	Men	Women
	%	%	%	%
Watching television	28	36	42	50
Doing jobs about the house	12	12	23	34
Following a hobby of some sort	19	24	18	23
Gardening	19	12	21	14
Reading newspapers and magazines	15	15	17	15
Reading books	14	19	13	17
Talking to family or friends	11	26	6	20
Going out to a pub	26	8	17	3
Going out to social activities	12	20	10	10
Playing sport	17	3	14	2
Going to watch sport	18	2	10	1
Dancing	3	10	2	4
Doing office work at home	—	—	3	1
Going out to the cinema	1	6	2	2
Doing nothing in particular	2	3	2	2

   a: Compare columns I and II. Why, in reference to 'Doing jobs about the house' are the figures much higher in Col. II than in Col. I?
   b: Why is this also so in regard to 'Watching television?'
   c: Find other activities where the reverse is true — Col. I higher than Col. II. In each case what do you think is the reason?
   d: What do you consider the most interesting activity in this list and why?
2. Make a list of teenage activities and work out a percentage chart for your class or group.

[64] LEISURE

3. The report on "Alcohol and Work" already quoted states that there are 740,000 people in the United Kingdom with serious drink problems. The cost to industry alone is enormous, reckoned at £100 million annually at the lowest and it could be much higher. Alcoholics lose on average 121.7 working days per year whereas the national average is 15.9. At work they become inefficient and are prone to accidents.
   What other ways of spending leisure time can be bad for health and work or cause inconvenience and annoyance to other people?
4. Getting to know people and making friends can be one of the greatest pleasures in life. Make a list of youth clubs and other organizations, such as scouts and guides, in your neighbourhood. Do you belong to any of them? If not, what reason have you against joining?
5. From your discussion of question 4 plan what you would consider to be an ideal club for young people in the area where you live.
6. Do you know any recreation, entertainment or other activity your local authority organises? Elect one of the class to write to the Council (if your library has not already got the information) and ask for details. You may be surprised as what you discover.
7. What have you read or seen on T.V. about the recreational activities of young people in other countries? Can we learn anything from them?
8. Many people find greater pleasure in reading than in anything else. Are you one of them? If not, has anyone really helped you to select books that you might like to read? You may easily be discouraged by the sight of thousands of books in a library, not knowing where to look for a book that will appeal to you. How can you overcome this difficulty?
9. Make a list of all the hobbies you have heard of. Which do you think is or might be most interesting? If you have a hobby or are thinking about one, do you know any person, book or evening class that could help you?
10. Aristotle, a famous Greek thinker, said 'The true aim of education is the right use of leisure.' How do you think day schools might help young people to employ their leisure time? Could you suggest a series of talks and excursions?
11. From your enquiries suggested in question 6 are there any other facilities you think the local council might provide for leisure time activities?
12. Why do you think religions generally seem to have very little to say about the use of leisure? What is necessary, do they teach, for the restoration of mind and body?

Some useful addresses

Are you interested in:
helping people?

> *Write to*
> Task Force,
> 1 Thorpe Close,
> London W10

parachute jumping or parascending?

> *Write to*
> The British Parachute Association,
> Kimberley House
> 47 Vaughan Way
> Leicester
> LE1 4SG

sports and outdoor life?

> *Write to*
> The Outward Bound Trust,
> 360 Oxford Street,
> London W1

sailing barges?

> *Write to*
> The Thames Barge Sailing Club,
> The National Maritime Museum,
> Romney Road,
> London SE10

Government

Where there is no vision the people perish.   Proverbs

The world is preserved by three things; truth, justice and peace.
Jewish Mishnah

To govern simply by statute and to maintain order by means of penalties is to render the people evasive and devoid of a sense of shame.   Confucius

Let good men manage a country for a century and crime will disappear.
Confucius

The essentials of a good government are a sufficiency of food, a sufficiency of arms, and the confidence of the people.   Confucius

Decisions on important matters should not be made by one person alone.
Shinto saying

He is fit to govern who loves all people as he loves himself.   Tao-te-King

Govern a large country as you would fry a small fish – without overdoing it.
Tao-te-King

The more prohibitions, the more poverty; the more laws, the more crimes; the more skills, the more luxuries; the more weapons, the more chaos.   Tao-te-King

The ideal land is small, its people few, its tools ten times or even a hundred times beyond their needs. These people live and die and never emigrate. They have weapons and armour that are never displayed. Their food is sweet; their clothes adorned; their houses at peace, and their customs full of charm. The neighbouring lands are so close that each may hear the other's crowing cocks and barking dogs. Yet men grow old and never once exchange a contentious call.   Tao-te-king

'There's always something to grumble about – if it isn't the weather, it's the government!' So many people, in fact, in so many countries grumble about politicians and blame the government for the state of their country, that you might very well ask, 'If governments are so unpopular, why do we have them at all?'

They are certainly very expensive. In Britain, for example, to make our system of government work we employ over 700,000 civil servants and 800,000 local government officers.

GOVERNMENT

It may seem absurd to suggest that we could do without government altogether, but there have always been people who argued seriously that government on the scale we know it is quite unnecessary.

One of the earliest was Li Urh, a Chinese, whose sayings you will find in the quotations under 'Tao-te-King.' He lived at a time when China was divided into separate states and the behaviour of the nobles who controlled them was so appalling that Li Urh despaired of government altogether. 'There has been such a thing as letting mankind alone; there has never been such a thing as governing mankind,' he declared.

Even when Confucius came along with laws for good government, he treated him as an interfering busybody. 'Leave people alone,' he said, 'and they will live at peace. The more laws, the more crimes; the more prohibitions, the more poverty.'

Anarchy is the modern name for this idea. The word means 'no-rule', and anarchists believe that government as we know it simply preserves the injustices and inequalities that exist, and that the rich use it to keep the vast fortunes they have made out of other people's labour. Get rid of it and oppression and force especially military force — will disappear.

Karl Marx, the founder of modern Communism, had similar ideas. In the final stage of the Communist Revolution central government would just 'wither away.'

What would happen then? People would be able to organise their lives together in much smaller groups where every man's opinion and vote would count for something. All kinds of associations would be formed — industrial, commercial, educational — to work together in friendly agreement.

One example of this today, is international travel. By voluntary agreements between nations we can travel almost anywhere by land, sea and air. Such friendly arrangements could be made to cover the whole of our life and work. There would then be no more conflict between government and governed, no more political prisoners and no more war between nations.

Unfortunately, the popular meaning of anarchy is disorder and confusion, since anarchists have often been associated with bomb throwing. They do, in fact, believe in violent revolution and therefore their ideas on government have rarely been considered seriously.

1. How would the anarchist idea apply to your school? Suppose there was no 'rule from the top,' and that each form ran its own affairs with various representatives from every form meeting to discuss matters that overlapped. Do you think such a system would work? What advantages and disadvantages would arise?

[68] GOVERNMENT

Head of Karl Marx on his tomb in Highgate Cemetary, London

    2.   Would such a system of control give you less or more interest in your school?

Abraham Lincoln defined the most popular form of government today, democracy, as government of the people by the people for the people.

Had you lived in Athens 2500 years ago you would have seen a fine example of it. All the citizens attended an Assembly in the market-place three times a month

GOVERNMENT [69]

and were paid their expenses for doing so. They could all speak and vote on the business of the city. They elected (by lot, to prevent corruption) their own officers to deal with day to day affairs, and everyone expected at some time to hold office.

If you compare the few thousand citizens who decided the affairs of Athens with the fifty million population of the United Kingdom you can see why our modern democracy doesn't work in the same way. Britain is divided into population areas called constituencies, and at every election in each of them candidates are voted for. Those who get the most votes are elected to Parliament. The most, therefore, that many citizens in Britain do towards the government of their own country is to pay their taxes and put a cross on a piece of paper say once every five years.

Here are the total figures for the 1979 election.

Total electorate: 41,093,264
Total votes cast: 31,222,279

Party	Votes cast	Percentage of total vote	Seats in Parliament
Conservative	13,697,753	43.9	339
Labour	11,509,524	36.9	268
Liberal	4,313,931	13.8	11
Communist	16,858	0.1	-
Welsh and Scottish Nationalists	636,803	2.0	4
Others	1,045,921	3.4	13

Some questions for the mathematicians in the class:

1. A Conservative government was formed as a result of the election. About what fraction of the total electorate voted for them?
2. On the percentage of votes cast, the Liberals should have had 87 seats. How many did they get? Work out, if you can, the number of seats the Nationalists and the Others should have had according to the votes cast.

You will have discovered that only a third of the total electorate put the government into power, and that many people's views were hardly represented at all (over six million in this election). This is often the case after a general election. Two other methods of voting have been suggested which would give a better

[70] GOVERNMENT

representation of the people. They are the Alternative Vote and Proportional Representation. But no government in power has ever yet considered a change. Why do you think this is?

If you are just one person among over forty million able to cast a vote, you may feel that your vote doesn't count for very much. In the election we have been studying nearly one out of every four of the electorate didn't vote. In council elections the fraction of non-voters is usually much higher. For example, in the Greater London Council elections of 1977 only 43.4% of the electors voted.

The British parliament is sometimes referred to as 'The Mother of Parliaments.' This is because the British democratic system dates back hundreds of years and other nations have based their own system of government upon it. It has provided steady government and a peaceful way of life in Britain for a very long time. It is just because of this that people are apt to take it for granted and to assume that it never can be altered or improved in any way.

1. List half a dozen reasons why people don't vote in elections. Are any of them justifiable?
2. What could happen if less and less people took an interest in politics?
3. What do you think could be done to make government *by* the people more effective?

But what of communism as a form of government? Over 1,400,000,000 people live under Communist rule — one third of the world population.

This system is really an alternative to capitalism, not to democracy, though no democratic communism exists anywhere in the world.

Communism is revolutionary socialism, and socialism is the belief that industry should no longer be in private hands for the benefit of the few but under public control for the benefit of everyone. Many people who accept this view believe that the change from private to public ownership can be brought about by act of parliament. Karl Marx said this was impossible. Real socialism could be achieved only by revolution — the violent overthrow of the capitalists. According to him there are three main stages in the change from capitalism to communism:

Revolution. All the workers unite and throw out the capitalists by force and take control themselves.

Provisional government. A period of a few years follows the revolution, during which the country becomes settled. While this is going on, leading communists who have seized power govern the country on behalf of the people.

The Communist State. All power will now be in the hands of the people. A classless society of complete equality and justice will appear. Central government will disappear and the control of life and work will be achieved by friendly agreements between the workers.

Russia has had communism for over sixty years, but stage 3, the Communist State, as Marx described it, has never come. Central government remains as strong as ever.

So, in fact, we have no democracy, as Lincoln defined it, in communist countries. Elections are held and the Russian government has often boasted that almost 100% of the people have voted. But they can vote only from prepared lists of communist party members. Only about one in twenty Russians belong to the party, so none of the other nineteen can stand as candidates. Government is in fact entirely in the hands of the privileged few.

Russia has made tremendous headway, perhaps because it is not a democracy. In half a century it raised 240,000,000 people from primitive poverty to a remarkable level of education and prosperity, and their country has become one of the most powerful in the world.

But to do this there has been a pitiless sacrifice of human life, which no democracy would ever tolerate. "East West Digest" for January 1980 gives the following death statistics:

1917–1924	Warfare, famine, organised killing	14,000,000
1918–1919	Maltreatment and murder in prisons	1,760,000
1932–1933	Organised starvation and murder of peasants	10,000,000
1918–1975	Slave labour camps	23,000,000

Wherever Communism has penetrated, for example, East Germany, Poland, Yugoslavia, Albania, Hungary, China, Tibet, North Korea, Indo-China, Cuba, Afghanistan, its progress has been marked by widespread inhuman slaughter. Accurate figures are clearly difficult to come by and those given above are only a fraction of the total. D.G. Stewart-Smith, editor of "East West Digest" estimated over ten years ago that the Marxist-Lenin experiment had already accounted for the death of between eighty and a hundred and twenty million people, great numbers of whom were murdered in cold blood.

After over sixty years of communist rule Russia remains a police state. People are still spied upon, their homes searched, themselves arrested, interrogated and detained for long periods. Imprisonment or forced labour is the penalty for criticising the government, as many writers, artists and people with religious convictions have discovered. If nothing worse befalls you, you may be confined to a hospital or sanatorium for drug treatment, since your views are considered a sign of mental derangement.

[72] GOVERNMENT

Similar things are happening in many non-communist countries. Torture and brutality towards political prisoners is widely practised. 'A concrete windowless tomb' is a description of a prominent political prisoner's cell, where he is being treated 'like a wild beast.'

Very many people are concerned about what is going on and one voluntary society, Amnesty International, has for twenty years devoted great efforts to helping these wretched victims of political persecution. It has a membership of a quarter of a million in 134 countries. Each year it deals with an average of 5000 individual cases of known or possible prisoners of conscience in more than seventy countries. In the course of three years recently 4,907 prisoners were released. Though Amnesty makes no direct claim for their release, there is no doubt that its influence in achieving it has been very considerable.

1. 'Russia has made tremendous headway, perhaps because it is not a democracy.' How would you explain this statement?
2. What do people mean when they say, 'The ends justify the means?' A Russian communist would probably say this about the recent history of his own country. Would you agree with him?

You may have noticed that there are no quotations from the New Testament at the head of this chapter. Jesus was no politician. When an eager crowd wanted to carry him off and make him King, he quickly disappeared. Throughout his lifetime an underground movement existed to overthrow the Roman rule. He took no part in it nor sided with any other political party.

Yet all government is judged by his standards. He taught that all men are God's children and as such they should enjoy equality and justice and share together the fruits of the earth. These are the standards which all countries claiming to be Christian must accept.

Christ would condemn much of what is going on in the world today. But what can be done about it? Here is an item of news:

RUSSIA LETS THE JEWS GO
A big exodus of Jews from Russia to Israel appears to be underway.

For very many years the Jews in Russia have been agitating for permission to leave the country. Their treatment by the Russian government has become widely

Manchester City Council in session

known and condemned. It is possible, therefore, that world opinion may have influenced this decision. However this may be, it is certainly true that governments do not like continued criticism and that, in the long run, they are influenced by public opinion:

Equality, justice and freedom. Vast numbers of people everywhere accept these ideals, but either they do not know what is going on in the world (if they live under dictatorships) or many of them feel quite helpless. 'What can anyone do?' they exclaim in despair. But doing something about it by every means possible is

[74] GOVERNMENT

partly what Christianity is about. Democracy can be made more democratic, tyranny can be overthrown — this is proved from the record of man's struggle for freedom down the centuries.

It is sometimes said that the Welfare State in Britain has made people lazy and indifferent. They are cared for by the State so thoroughly from cradle to grave that they no longer concern themselves about anything but their own private affairs. This is not a true picture of society.

Politicians are paid for their work; they do a full-time job. But in Britain there are many thousands of people who give their services willingly to help run the country. Magistrates, councillors, governors of hospitals, schools, charities, public and private institutions; people caring for the sick, the aged, the young, the countryside, animals and wildlife — the list is unending. Churches raise large sums of money for charities and good causes and provide a reservoir of service to the community.

Without the continuous help of these public spirited citizens life in Britain would be much poorer. It is, in fact, doubtful whether government and good order could survive without them.

So apart from the international scene and its problems, there is much we can all do at home to help community life in addition to casting our vote at each general election.

Mahatma Gandhi said, 'A society's civilisation should not be judged by its powers over the forces of nature, nor by the powers of its literature and art, but by the gentleness and kindness of its members towards all living things.'

Passages from the Bible for further study

Romans 13, 1–10	Paul's attitude to the Roman government
Matthew 10, 28	Faith and conscience more important than life
Mark 12, 13–17	What did Christ mean?

For Discussion

1. What advantages has dictatorship over democracy? Would you ever like to see a dictatorship in your country? Think out your answer carefully and give your reasons.

GOVERNMENT [75]

2. What do you think are the advantages and disadvantages of 'The Welfare State?'
3. Write to
   a: Amnesty International,
      Tower House, Southampton Street, London WC2
   and
   b: The National Council for Civil Liberties,
      186 King's Cross Road, London, WC1
   and ask them for information about the work they are doing. Give a report to the class and consider any ways in which you can help.
4. 'Half of the people who have got the vote don't use it and most of the other half vote for the same old party every time. They don't know what they are voting for.' Do you agree with this criticism? Why does the speaker think people don't know what they are voting for?
5. Do you think there should be more political parties? What would be the advantages and disadvantages
6. Make a list of three or four urgent problems that you think the government should deal with. Against each one say what you think ought to be done. Your answers could lead to some good class discussion.
7. In this country do you think there is 'one law for the rich and another for the poor?' How do you justify your answer?
8. With help from your library write a short history of communism in Russia. What do you consider are the good and bad points about communism?
9. What does the word 'patriotism' mean? Is there any place for patriotism in our present-day world?
10. If you were a local councillor, what improvements would you suggest to the council for your neighbourhood? What can anyone do who is not a councillor to draw attention to these things?
11. If you are able, invite a local councillor or magistrate to come to school to talk about his work.
12. 'I detest your ideas but I am ready to die for your right to express them.' (Voltaire) Do you think anyone should be allowed to express any ideas anywhere? In what circumstances is this not permitted in Britain? Do you agree with these restrictions?
13. Get a copy of the Universal Declaration of Human Rights (from your library or from the United Nations London Information Centre, 14 Stratford Place, London W1); write out Articles 5, 9, 18, 19 and discuss them in class.

Sex and marriage

A man shall leave his father and mother and be made one with his wife, and the two shall become one flesh. It follows that they are no longer two individuals: they are one flesh. What God has joined together man must not separate.
Jesus

You have learnt that they (the Israelites under Moses) were told, 'Do not commit adultery.' But what I tell you is this: If a man looks on a woman with a lustful eye, he has already committed adultery with her in his heart.   Jesus

As rain breaks through an ill-thatched roof, so lust breaks through an ill-trained mind.   Buddhist saying

Passion is the slave or mistress; followed she will bring but sorrow; lead her, and you tread the path of fortune.   Hindu saying

He who is carried away by passion will not get very far.   Jain saying

Three things the superior man guards against: lusts of the flesh in youth, combativeness in maturity, and ambition in old age.   Confucius

Love is from God; anyone who loves is a child of God.
There is no room for fear in love; perfect love banishes fear.   John

It is better to marry than burn.   Paul

Honour your wife and your life will be enriched.   Jewish Talmud

> 'ARE WE THE LAST MARRIED GENERATION?'   Sunday paper
>
> *I was married once. Now I live with a man and we are very happy together. Marriage is out of date, that is unless you want to have children, and the world is overpopulated as it is.*   Hollywood actress
>
> *Being married and having children is a dull business. Let's have fun first.*
> Teenage boy
>
> *You'll find that* everybody *has sex before marriage now-a-days.*   Young woman now married and expecting her first baby

Though at least two statements in the above quotations are untrue, this is how many people are thinking and talking today. The rigid old rules about sex and marriage are under fire. Everybody discusses them and many people reject them.

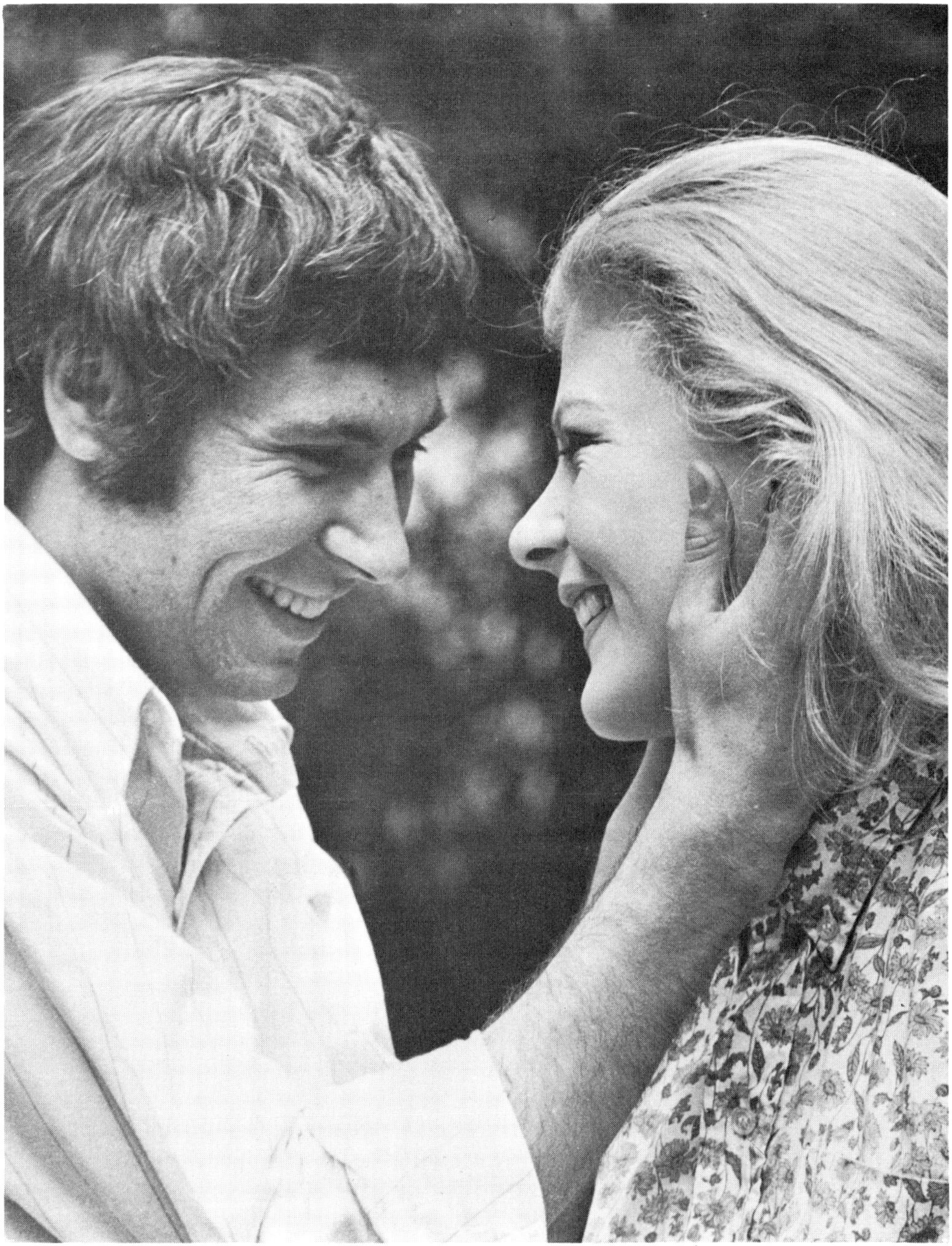

[78] SEX AND MARRIAGE

Sex before marriage? Of all questions this is the most discussed. Is it right or wrong, wise or foolish?

In the first place, this is a decision you must make for yourself. It is far too important to be settled simply by what your friends do or by statements such as 'Everybody does it' or by T.V. plays and novels that assume that it is the natural thing to do.

In real life, how many people do have sex before marriage? One psychologist said that of all the questions put to young people this was the most unreliably answered.

However, a less personal question was put to a group of a hundred young people: Do you approve of having sex before marriage? Here are their answers:

	For	Against
(1) Where no affection	19	81
(2) When you like the person	41	59
(3) When you are in love	69	31
(4) When you are engaged	84	16

Though many people object to sex before marriage for religious or practical reasons others argue that:

1. Those who have it are likely to get along better when they are married because of their previous experience.

2. When two people are seriously in love and have prospects of marriage, to live together for a while will help them considerably to make a final decision.

In Scotland and Denmark until recent times there was a custom called "Handfasting". Once a couple had pledged themselves to each other while holding hands they were allowed to live together for a year and a day. Then either their marriage would take place or they would be free. But if there was a child, it should be supported by the partner who objected to the marriage.

In certain parts of the West Indies it was a fairly common practice for two people to live together and save up for a big marriage ceremony, possibly after some years when they could afford it.

In both these examples living together was accepted as a serious business and the intention was to marry later.

This, of course, is quite different from casual sex which few young people seem to approve of. Here are three reasons why people disapprove of it:

1. In the last thirty years with the Permissive Society has come a great increase in the spread of venereal disease. Many thousands of people — mainly between

SEX AND MARRIAGE

18 and 24 — contract it each week and nearly half a million cases are dealt with in hospital each year — treble the number of thirty years ago.

2. Contraceptives are not 100% fool-proof and, in any case, it is estimated that less than a third of unmarried girls having intercourse use them. Between 55% and 75% do not use them in their first experience. In America, for instance, it is estimated that a million 15-19 year old girls become pregnant every year. In Britain, with a much smaller population, over 5000 school girls under 16 become pregnant every year ("Nationwide" 25.1X.80).

3. "Sex for the fun of it — it's just a bore," said a young man who had done a good deal of 'sleeping around'. He meant, of course, that the glamour and romance fade and the act becomes mechanical and loveless.

1: Why are teenagers' answers to the question as to whether they have 'had sex' unreliable?

2: Read again the quotations at the head of this chapter. Quite a number are warnings. What are they warning us against? Why is this necessary?

From answering the second question you will have discovered that religions make a distinction between love and lust. It is an important one and both civilized and uncivilized communities base their rules for sex upon it. These rules are necessary for their very survival, because the sex urge is one of the most powerful of man's instincts and given free rein can wreck society.

Even people who opt out of society and set up little communities of their own have to lay down strict rules about sex, otherwise life together becomes impossible.

Married couples who accept no religious beliefs to guide them have to make their own rules and keep them if they are going to live happily together. They have to accept a good deal of self-control. 'Wife-swopping' and other permissive experiments in married life are not usually successful!

A civilization's rules on sex and marriage are based on its religion. Our western civilization is based on Christianity, and Christian teaching is sometimes condemned by people who have never really bothered to understand it. For example, nowhere does Jesus suggest that sex and marriage are subjects which are 'hush-hush' or vaguely unclean. On the contrary, he talks quite openly about them and would expect us to do the same, but he lays down rules which require a high standard of self-control and consideration for other people.

His teaching has mainly to do with marriage. It assumes that the sex act is an expression of deep and intimate love between two people. One person should never use another as a piece of apparatus to satisfy a selfish desire. Love, someone has said, is what is left when passion and desire are exhausted. And if there is nothing left, then in these circumstances the sex act is wrong.

There was also a permissive section of society in Christ's day. One distinguished Jewish rabbi taught that a man could divorce his wife for the most trivial reasons: if she was a bad cook or if he found someone else he liked better.

Jesus said this was wrong. He declared that the only grounds for divorce could be unfaithfulness. Whether he laid down this rule for all time we do not know, but we do know that he taught that married life should be governed absolutely by love, and that it could and should be permanent. 'What God has joined together, man must not separate.'

If you are married in church this is the vow you will take:

> I call upon these persons here present to witness that I do take thee to be my lawful wedded wife (husband), to have and to hold from this day forward, for better for worse, for richer for poorer, in sickness and in health, to love and to cherish, till death us do part according to God's holy law: and thereto I give thee my troth (promise).

Among practising Christians, therefore, marriage is a solemn contract, or sacrament, undertaken consciously in the presence of God by two people who should have learnt enough about each other to feel sure that their love will cope with all the problems of living together.

It is generally a success because the people concerned are under oath to make it so. They will keep their vows and practise the love towards each other that Christ expects of them. 'Those that pray together, stay together.'

The 'broken home' rarely occurs, therefore, in Christian marriage. Any alternative system should at least safeguard children from being unwanted or becoming the helpless victims of quarrelling parents.

Passages from the Bible for further study

Deuteronomy 22, 13–20	Sex relations – the Old Law
Deuteronomy 24, 1–5	Divorce – the Old Law
Deuteronomy 5, 18	The Seventh Commandment
Proverbs 7, 6–23	The folly of yielding to the wiles of a prostitute
Mark 10, 2–12	Christian marriage
Matt. 5, 27–32	Adultery and divorce

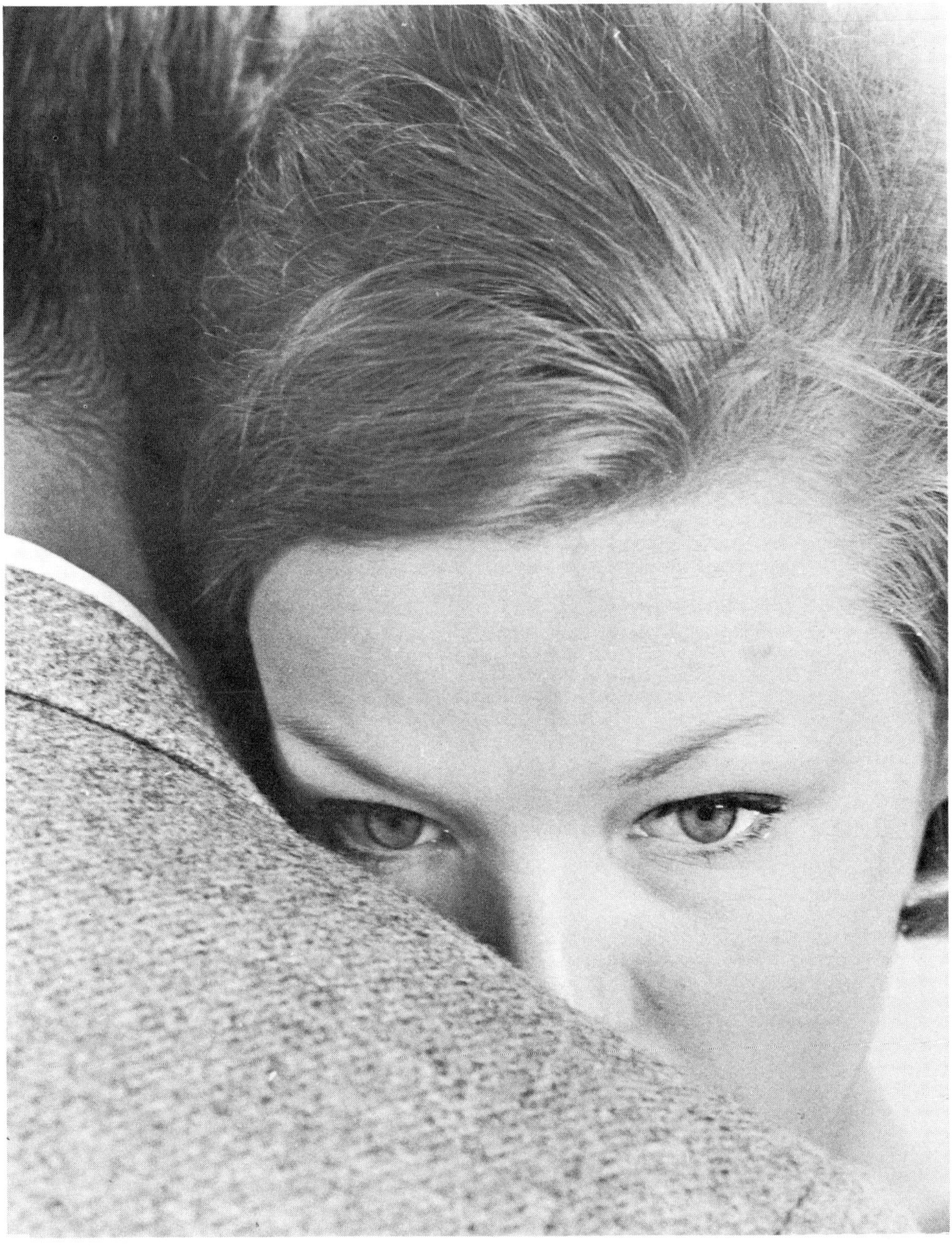

[82] SEX AND MARRIAGE

John 8, 2–12	Christ and the adulteress – the New Law
I Corinthians 13, 4–7	True love
Ephesians 5, 22–33	Paul's advice to husbands and wives

For Discussion

1. Here is some research to do:
   1: What is 'the age of consent?'
   2: At what age can you get married
      a: without your parent's consent
      b: with your parent's consent?
   3: In what circumstances can two people get divorced?
   4: How does a legal separation differ from a divorce? Has it any advantages over divorce?
   5: In what circumstances is abortion legal?
2. What is the difference between infatuation and love?
3. Falling in and out of love with different members of the opposite sex can make life very difficult. What difficulties and inconveniences does it create? If we are going to get the best out of life, how should we deal with them?
4. Boys want sex; girls want marriage. True or false?
5. Over a number of years statistics show that in America 40% of brides were between 15 and 18 and one out of two of them was divorced within five years; in Britain 21% were between 15 and 18 and one out of four were divorced within five years. Do you think that these marriage breakdowns matter? Is it true that girls are eager to get married however young they are while boys would much prefer to wait?
6. Is sexual intercourse before marriage wrong in all circumstances? Give reasons for your answer.
7. What qualities would you look for in your partner in order to make a successful marriage? Here is an assortment. Choose those that appeal to you or any others you can think of and write them down in order of importance, if you can.
    brains, good looks, good manners, comradeship, passionate love, considerateness, sense of humour, same interests, same religion, same social

SEX AND MARRIAGE [83]

class, same age, good health, physical strength, tallness (shortness), good figure, wealth, sexual compatibility.

The results should make an interesting class discussion.

8. Should people who do not profess to be Christian be married in church?
9. To become a wife or husband is possibly the most serious job a man or woman can undertake. As with other jobs, training is essential. What training have you had or do you hope to have for married life? Does your sex education in school really help? Are there any improvements you could seriously suggest?
10. Discuss sex
    a: on T.V. and in films
    b: in books and magazines.
    Is there too much of it? Are there features of it you dislike? Do you believe in any kind of censorship? Write down what changes you would make to benefit the community if you were dictator.
11. In some countries people can be married in hotels, private houses or some other place which they choose. Is this a good idea?
12. 'You start hot and grow cold; we start cold and grow warm.' This was a comment on Western marriage by a girl who comes from a country where marriages are arranged by parents and falling in love plays little or no part in them. She obviously meant that the custom of her country made for more successful marriages. What do you think about this?
13. As an alternative to question 7 write a composition — anonymous if desired — on 'My Ideal Wife (Husband),' Your teacher might collect the compositions, list the main points you make and discuss them in class.

Religion

Men who have not led a religious life die like herons on a lake without fish.
Buddhism

*Man shall not live by bread alone but by every word
that proceedeth out of the mouth of God.*   Jesus

The speculations of agnostics cannot lead to knowledge.   Jainism

*The fear of the Lord makes a merry heart and gives joy
and gladness and a long life.*   Judaism

Religion is like rain: when it falls on good soil, it causes fresh grass to grow.
Islam

*As He was in the beginning the Truth, So throughout the ages He has been the
Truth, So even now He is Truth all-pervading, So for ever and ever He shall be the
Truth eternal.*   Sikh meditation

A pious man eats little, drinks little, sleeps little.   Jainism

Trust in God, but tie your camel.   Islam

*He who hates nothing of all that lives, himself compassionate, free from arrogance
and love of self, unchanged by good or ill; patient, contented, firm in faith,
master of himself, true to his word, seeking me (Krishna), heart and soul; vowed
to me – that man I love.*   Hinduism

True religion is to love, as God has loved them, all things whether great or small.
Hinduism

'I don't believe in all that lark,' said a girl in a recent television play talking about religion. Perhaps you don't believe in it, either. But many people do, and most people have fairly strong views one way or the other. This is because religion is one of the most powerful influences in human life and cannot be ignored.

Here are the figures for the main world religions:

Hindus	500 million	Jews	13½ million
Buddhists	300 million	Christians	1200 million

RELIGION [85]

| Muslims | 600 million | Primitive beliefs | 100 million |
| Taoists / Shinto | 93 million | | |

These figures can be only a rough guide but they remind us that religion is worldwide. It has dominated all the known history of man back to the earliest records of pre-history.

Most religions have suffered persecution many times but they survive all attempts to destroy them. In 1917 the Russian government began an intensive anti-God campaign. They set out to show that religion was untrue, unnecessary and absurd. But they gave up their main propoganda after some years because it was having the reverse effect from what they intended. Today Muslims, Jews and Christians still practise their religion in Russia, though they continually suffer for it.

Where the communists have succeeded in bringing up children as atheists there is a curious development. In Russia you have the 'worship' of Lenin and in China for many years the 'worship' of Mao. In fact, communism, like the old religions, has its sacred writings, its commandments and its promised paradises. It seems that man is not quite himself unless he has a religion of some kind to follow.

What do the main religions of the world teach? With certain exceptions they agree on four important points. They believe in

1: A supreme Being, or Beings, responsible for man's existence and concerned about his welfare.
2: Some form of survival after death dependent on the way we have behaved in life.
3: A spiritual world to be discovered by self-discipline in meditation and prayer.
4: A high standard of behaviour towards our fellowmen.

Hinduism and Buddhism show some variation of the first belief. The highest form of Hinduism, instead of a personal god, teaches that there is a Universal Essence in all creation of which man's soul is a part. The oldest form of Buddhism, though not denying God's existence, teaches that man can find salvation (Nirvana) only within himself. But the vast majority of Hindus and Buddhists believe in supernatural beings.

Sacred writings, or scriptures, are found in all religions except those of primitive people. They were composed many centuries ago. The most recent are the Adi Granth (Sikh) in the 16th century and the Koran (Muslim) in the 7th century.

[86] RELIGION

Does their age make them out of date? Not as seriously as we might think, because they are mainly concerned with human nature which does not change. The kind of people, for example, that Jesus met and talked about can be seen today with exactly the same virtues and failings. But it does mean that these scriptures have to be carefully studied, usually with the help of a teacher who can explain their background. This is certainly true of the Christian Bible about which a great deal of nonsense is talked by people ignorant of its contents and uninformed about its writers.

'Religion has caused a lot of trouble in the world!' It most certainly has, mainly because its teachings have been abused. You can, if you search carefully, find a text in the scriptures to justify almost any action you care to take. So the most brutal wars have been fought in the name of religion and it has been used to justify terrible cruelties and savage persecution.

This is all the more sad because the founders of the great religions taught love, compassion and forgiveness, and many of their followers in every generation have tried faithfully to practise their teaching.

> *The more you mow us down the more we grow.*   Tertullian
> Why has it proved useless to try to suppress religion?

> *Different religions are but different paths that lead to God.*   Rama Krishna
> Do you agree or do you think Christianity teaches there is only one path?

'But things are different now; we don't need religion any more. We've outgrown it.' This is a point of view held by some people, chiefly modern humanists, who also add that religion requires faith and today we should live by reason alone.

Man, not God, should now take the centre of the stage. Science and sociology can solve all man's problems for him. This was the view of a French humanist, Auguste Comte, and two of his friends actually founded a church in England for the worship of Man.

Things are certainly different now. In the last fifty years man has made more scientific progress than during the whole of his previous history on earth. We are told, for instance, that ninety percent of all the scientists whoever lived, are alive today.

In the west our standards of living are going up and up. More and more people live in comfort and even luxury compared with their grandparents. Every year there are more motor cars, television sets, labour saving devices in the home, better houses, longer holidays, shorter working hours, more foreign travel, more trips into space. Doctors have conquered diseases that killed people a generation ago. Soon the organs of our bodies, as they wear out, will be neatly replaced by excellent second-hand ones, and we shall no doubt discover how to go on living for centuries. The future is very bright.

It should be, but is it? Think for a moment of those disturbing problems we push to the back of our minds: the H bomb, pollution, the Cold War, racial hatreds, famine, the ghastly poverty of over half the human race. As we have seen earlier in this book (World Poverty) it is, in fact, seriously argued, that our much talked of progress is really downhill, and that man is heading towards his own destruction.

Remember the Creation story? 'And God looked upon everything that he had made and behold it was very good.' If the good life was God's intention for mankind, it seems that man has lost his way.

What we certainly need, as a human family, is a sense of direction and a very much greater compassion for one another if we are going to survive. But this is exactly what a sincere faith in God offers to man, and before we talk about discarding religion, we should ask ourselves what real alternative there is to it. 'Unless we learn to live together as brothers,' said Martin Luther King, 'we shall all perish together as fools.'

There is something else about our modern world that is very disturbing. The richer we grow, the more harassing life seems to become.

Charles Clark, Chairman of the National Association for Mental Health, in "Simple Faith", stated that nearly forty million working days a year are lost through people being off work with mental illness and each year five million patients go to their doctor with symptoms of stress, anxiety and some kind of neurotic state. Four thousand people in England succeed in killing themselves each year and about forty thousand attempt suicide unsuccessfully. One in six women and one in nine men will at some time during their lives enter a psychiatric hospital for treatment, and it is estimated that more than half of all the hospital beds in the country are occupied by people with some form of mental disorder.

And for every one in hospital there are many more people who 'keep themselves going' by such devices as tranquilisers, tobacco and alcohol. This is an age of drug taking, both on and off prescription. What is the answer to this problem of increasing tension in modern society? A man's greatest problem in life is himself. How can he overcome the worries, anxieties and frustrations that beset him?

Here again religion claims to give the answer. Dr. Jung, one of the most famous psychologists of modern times, said, 'During the last thirty years, people from all civilized countries of the earth have consulted me. . . . Among my patients over

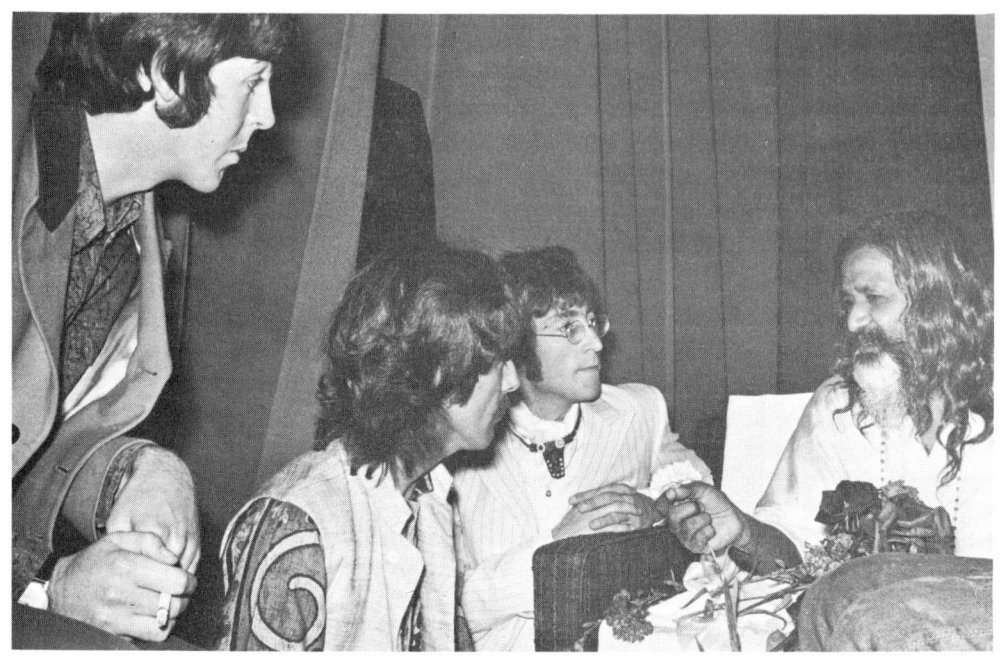

Members of the former pop group The Beatles with the Maharishi

Some of a group of 1800 Buddhist schoolgirls who meditate for one hour each morning

35 years of age, there has not been one whose problem in the last resort has not been that of finding a religious outlook on life. Everyone of them fell ill because he had lost that which the living religions of every age have given their followers, and not one of them has been really healed who did not regain his religious outlook'

But what of people under 35? The late John Lennon, one of the Beatles, wrote, 'The youth of today are looking for some answers.... the Established church can't give them, their parents can't give them, material things can't give them.' The Beatles, you will remember, reached well beyond the goal in life so many people desire — enormous success and unlimited wealth. Yet they turned to religion — the Hindu mystic, Maharishi Marash — in the hope of finding an answer to the vital questions of life.

Of course, the religions of the world do answer very important questions. Look again at the four principal beliefs on p. 84. If you do, in fact, believe in God, in a future life and in the immense importance of everything you do in this one, life has very real meaning for you. And meditation and prayer do relieve the strain of daily life and give peace of mind. Many Buddhists, for example, will spend up to an hour in meditation before they begin their day's work.

Do you think young people are happy to accept life as it is lived by older people? If not, what do they feel is lacking? What are they looking for?

'We don't know if it's true!' said a thirteen year old boy when asked why he and some of his friends did not believe in God.

This is possibly the greatest difficulty of all for young people. They are brought up to doubt. Organised religion does not appeal to them, the Scriptures are rarely if ever read, and life goes on quite happily with good health, a good job, plenty of money, and a comfortable home where religion is never mentioned. Yet there are doubts and dissatisfactions. Is this all life consists of? Has it no meaning or purpose? Are we just a conglomeration of atoms? Is man's sole destiny 'a grinning skull at the end of the road?'

Young people sample meditation, faith-healing, yoga, mysticism, witchcraft, hypnotism, spiritualism, astrology, telepathy. The list grows, simply because deep within us all there is a feeling that the riddle of life can be answered.

Perhaps the teaching of Jesus, for example, could be the answer, if only we could believe it. If only there were proof?

But how much proof is there of anything else? We live our daily life on probability, not proof. The desk upon which this manuscript has been written is a mystery, for the more we analyse matter the more blurred becomes our understanding of it. We exist on theories: evolution, the nature of matter, the origin of the universe. Society depends on political and economic theories. There are so

A section of the large congregation that worships each Sunday at All Souls, Langham Place, London

many things about which we know so little, yet we manage to live by using what we cannot explain or understand.

Lord Kelvin, the famous scientist, once asked a student in an oral examination, 'What is electricity?' The student hesitated, blushed and then blurted out, 'I'm sorry, sir. I did know, but I've forgotten.' 'What a pity,' replied Lord Kelvin. 'The whole world is waiting for you to remember.'

We can't explain electricity but that doesn't prevent us from pressing the switch and using the light and power it produces.

This kind of experiment is all that religious teachers ask of us. We know there are many questions about God and the future life that cannot be explained. All they say to us is this: accept the fact of God, act upon it, and the results will come. 'Ask and you will receive, seek and you will find, knock and the door will be opened.' Press the switch – and the light will come.

"This, of course, is true. Within the last ten years, for example, a new experience in religion has sprung up in America – The Jesus Movement. Thousands of young people formed about 600 communes where they lived together. They were united in the one claim that Jesus had completely changed their lives. Great numbers of them been hopeless victims of drugs and alcohol and had been cured, without any withdrawal symptoms, by faith.

More recently the Movement has changed in form, splitting up into many groups in different parts of the country. But their lifestyle remains basically the same. They live a simple disciplined life: their rule book, the Bible: their aim, Christian comradeship. Speaking of life outside the commune, one young man declared, "Out there I found everything I wanted except love. I felt that it did not exist. Here it is all around me".

This kind of approach to religion may not appeal to us at all, and this particular movement may decline. But there are many other ways in which men find that faith in God has a real answer to life's problems.

Passages from the Bible for further study

Matt. 25, 31–46	Religion means action
John 3, 16	Christianity in a sentence
Romans 8, 28	Not chance but design
Luke 17, 20, 21	Here and now!
Mark 8, 35–38	The sacrifice of the greater for the less
James 1, 19–27	True religion

WANTED

JESUS CHRIST

ALIAS: THE MESSIAH, SON OF GOD, KING OF KINGS, LORD OF LORDS, PRINCE OF PEACE, ETC.

★ Notorious Leader of an underground liberation movement

★ Wanted for the following charges:
   — Practicing medicine, wine-making and food distribution without a license.
   — Interfering with businessmen in the Temple.
   — Associating with known criminals, radicals, subversives, prostitutes, and street people.
   — Claiming to have the authority to make people into God's children.

★ APPEARANCE: Typical hippie type — long hair, beard, robe, sandals, etc.

★ Hangs around slum areas, few rich friends, often sneaks out into the desert.

★ Has a group of disreputable followers, formerly known as "apostles," now called "freemen" (from his saying: "You will know the truth and the Truth will set you free.")

BEWARE — This man is extremely dangerous. His insidiously inflammatory message is particularly dangerous to young people who haven't been taught to ignore him yet. He changes men and claims to set them free.

WARNING: HE IS STILL AT LARGE!

Part of a Jesus Movement poster

RELIGION [93]

For Discussion

1. Find out
   a: The Four Noble Truths of Buddhism.
   b: The Five Pillars of the Faith in Islam.
   c: The Two Commandments of Christianity.
   Discuss the differences you find here between the three religions. Is there any common ground on which the followers of each religion can unite?
2. Why should anyone feel obliged to live a good life?
3. If God is good why does he allow so many people to suffer from natural calamities such as earthquakes, floods and hurricanes?
4. 'A man's greatest problem in life is himself.' What does this mean?
5. What is wrong with man that he causes so much unnecessary suffering in the world?
6. Can we hope for a world-wide brotherhood of man without believing in the fatherhood of God? Give your reasons.
7. What has Christianity in common with Communism? In what ways does it differ?
8. 'Religion and politics don't mix.' What is meant by this statement? Is it true?
9. What is wrong with the Christian Church? Do you agree with a recent survey among young people many of whom declared that church people are 'stuck-up snobs who keep themselves to themselves' 'middle-aged, stodgy and self-important,' or 86% who thought the need was not for formal instruction but for a chance to discuss things sensibly with other Christians?
10. An American doctor recently claimed that going to Church on a Sunday is good for both body and soul. Church going and the clean living that goes with it help people to avoid a variety of physical ills. Do you agree with this view? If you do would you say it was a sufficient reason for church going?
11. What religious items have you seen or heard on T.V. or radio? What were they about? What did you think of them? How could they be improved?
12. Name three or four denominations in the Christian Church. What do you know about any one of them? Do you think having different denominations is a good idea?
13. If you were given an unlimited supply of money with which to build a centre for religion in your neighbourhood, how would you design and use such a centre?

Examination questions

Family

1. Why do many Christians believe that family life as we know it is the best way of organising society? Are there any other kinds of "family" which can be run on Christian principles? Give your views.
   East Anglian Examinations Board

2. 'I can't do anything with him.' What is wrong in a home when a mother or father says this of a teenage son? What has Christianity to offer for wholesome family life?
   East Anglian Examinations Board

3. Either a: (i) What do you consider are the *four* most important needs of the aged?
   (ii) How can these needs be met?

   OR b: (i) Some old people die of neglect. Explain how such tragedies occur.
   (ii) Give your ideas on how such tragedies can be prevented.
   Southern Regional Examinations Board

4. a: Give the name of an organisation which exists to help one-parent families.
   b: Why do some families have only one parent? Give *three* of the usual reasons.
   c: Is it harder for a father to bring up a family single-handed than a mother?
   (i) Give your views on this question.
   (ii) Explain why the question is often important when a judge must decide on the custody or care of children.
   d: In what ways can the churches help one-parent families?
   East Anglian Examinations Board

5. Give some reasons for trouble developing:
   a: Between parents and children in the home.
   b: Between the children themselves.
   What teaching in the Bible is aimed at improving family relationships?
   East Midland Regional Examinations Board

[96] EXAMINATION QUESTIONS

World Poverty

1. What is Christian Aid? Describe how it is organised in this country and how it is applied abroad.
   London Regional Examining Board

2. What are some of the reasons that Christians feel it their duty to relieve suffering in far-off lands. Give examples.
   East Anglian Examinations Board

3. Either a: (i) Make a list of the ways in which world poverty occurs.
   (ii) How can world poverty be prevented or eased?
   OR b: What do you think Christians should do about world poverty and underprivilege? Illustrate your answer with examples of what is being done.
   Southern Regional Examinations Board

Money

1. 'Seek ye first the Kingdom of God and his righteousness and all these things shall be added unto you.' Give the teaching of Jesus in that section of the Sermon on the Mount which led to this pronouncement.
   West Yorkshire and Lindsey Regional Examining Board

2. 1 Timothy 6: 9-10 states that "The love of money is the root of all evil things . . ."
   a: Give an example from the teaching of Jesus of the misuse of money (or riches or possessions).
   b: Give a different example from the teaching of Jesus where the right use of money is praised.
   c: Make positive suggestions how Christians should use their money in the modern world. Give reasons for your answer.
   Southern Regional Examinations Board

3. A group of young people, some with small children, start to live together in a large house. No one is allowed to have more possessions than anyone else.
   a: Give reasons for and against this way of life.
   b: How would a religious person answer one of this group who said that marriage was unnecessary?
   East Midland Regional Examinations Board

4. Choose two of the following and explain what each means and state the Christian attitude towards each:
   (i): Money talks.
   (ii): It's the lolly that counts.
   (iii): You can't take it with you.
   East Anglian Examinations Board

5. a: Would having all the possessions we want make life perfect? Give reasons for your answer.
   b: How did Jesus reply to the man who said, "Master tell my brother to divide the family property with me"?
   c: What difference does a religious faith make in the search for happiness?
   London Regional Examining Board

Race

1. Miss A, a white girl, married Mr. X, a coloured man, who had shown himself kind, considerate and understanding. Her parents are hostile and the neighbours are critical, but the local Church where they worship regularly is friendly. Has this marriage any chance of success? Give your reasons.
   East Midland Regional Examination Board

2. a: What is the meaning of:
      (i) apartheid,
      (ii) colour,
      (iii) racial prejudice?
   b: Give an example to support each of your definitions.
   c: What is the Christian attitude towards each of these problems?
   d: How do Galatians 3 vv. 26 and 28 summarise the Christian point of view?
   East Anglian Examinations Board

3. Either a: Some groups of foreign people tend to keep to themselves in one area. Explain the reasons for this and show how the church could help integration.
   OR b: (i) Give your ideas of why immigrants come to settle in this country. Are there any religious problems? If so, discuss the difficulties.

[98] EXAMINATION QUESTIONS

(ii) Explain what could happen if there were no barriers to people moving into another country.

Southern Regional Examination Board

Work

1. a: In choosing a career what importance would you give to each of the following points? Give your reasons.
   - (i) Your interest in the actual work.
   - (ii) Pay.
   - (iii) Hours and conditions of work.
   - (iv) Security and pensions prospects.
   - (v) Chances of promotion.

   b: What further considerations might a Christian wish to take into account?

   c: What kinds of occupation do you consider a Christian ought not to accept and why?

   Associated Lancashire Schools Examining Board

2. Either a: (i) Some church leaders think that Christian principles should be worked out in industry. What principles would you think they want to see?
   (ii) From your list agree or disagree with the working of the principles in practice.

   OR b: (i) Give a brief account of *four* bad practices you know about in industry.
   (ii) Show from the teaching of Jesus what is wrong with the bad practices you have chosen.

   Southern Regional Examination Board

3. In what situations might a modern Christian with a job in industry find it hard to stick to his or her principles?
   Mention any New Testament teaching which might help in these difficulties.

   East Anglian Examinations Board

4. a: What does St. Paul say (in 2 Thessalonians) about people of "idle habits"?

   b: Why is unemployment generally regarded as an evil to be prevented?

EXAMINATION QUESTIONS [99]

   c: What kind of work do you hope to do when you leave school? How do you think that your religious faith would influence your attitude to the work you have chosen?

London Regional Examining Board

War and violence

1. 'Nation shall not lift up sword against nation nor ever again be trained for war' (Isaiah 2 v.4).
   a: Why do many people believe that Britain still needs a professional army "trained for war"?
   b: What Christian arguments could be used for and against this view?
   East Anglian Examinations Board

2. Either a: (i) Explain what is meant by "using violence".
   (ii) Give *three* examples of the use of violence in the world.
   (iii) Discuss ways in which violence might be contained or even prevented.
   OR b: (i) Jesus said, "All who take the sword will perish by the sword". What do you think he meant by this statement?
   (ii) Discuss the Christian attitude to violence.
   Southern Regional Examination Board

3. Have I ever a duty to defend others by the use of force? Describe
   a: an imaginary situation in which you consider a person to be fully justified in using force to protect someone else.
   b: a set of circumstances in which the use of force would not be justified.
   East Anglian Examinations Board

4. "If God is love, why is there so much suffering in the world?"
   How might a Christian answer this question?
   East Anglian Examinations Board

5. What are the 'rights' and 'responsibilities' of a pacifist?
   East Anglian Examinations Board

6. a: What did Jesus tell us we should do:
   (i) If someone sues us for a coat?
   (ii) If someone forces us to make a journey of a mile?
   (iii) If someone wants to borrow from us?

EXAMINATION QUESTIONS

b: Jesus said, 'if anyone struck you on the right cheek you should offer him the left cheek also'. What does this mean?

East Anglian Examinations Board

Leisure

1. In what ways do people offer voluntary service to others? You may confine your answer, if you wish, to the work of young people. Is such work a real Christian duty or only a social matter?

   London Regional Examining Board

2. Either a: (i) Discuss the proper and improper use of drugs.
   (ii) Explain *three* of the following terms:
   addiction, overdose, trip, hallucinations, tolerance, pusher.

   OR b: (i) The public is being taught, "Do not drink and drive". Why is such teaching necessary?
   (ii) What do you think the church should do about the problem of drunkenness?

   Southern Regional Examination Board

3. People today have an increasing amount of leisure time.
   a: What does the Bible tell us about the ways in which Jesus used his leisure time?
   b: Suggest *three* ways in which a Christian might use leisure time.
   c: What subjects might be included in an "Education for leisure" course for school leavers?

   East Anglian Examinations Board

Government

1. Read Mark 12, 13-17
   a: Explain in your own words the teaching of Jesus to this clever question.
   b: How is it possible for a Christian to serve God and respect the Head of State in countries where religious people are persecuted?
   c: Is authority always right? What kind of authority do you most respect?

   Southern Regional Examination Board

2. Political persecution is carried out in several African States. Such a practice is being excused as being a necessary stage in the emergence of true democracy.
   a. What is political persecution?
   b. Could you defend such a practice in Britain?
   Give reasons for your answer.
   East Midland Regional Examinations Board
3. It is said that the duty of every man is 'to leave the world a better place than he found it.' How does a Christian set about putting this ideal into practice and what problems — social and personal — will he expect to meet and overcome? *East Anglian Examinations Board*
4. a: State *three* rights which a citizen has in this country.
   b: People often say "It's a free country", but our actions are limited by the law. State three examples of people not being allowed to do what they like.
   c: Is it true to say that a Christian has a duty:
      (i) to vote?
      (ii) to be a member of a trade union?
      (iii) to take an active part in the social life of the community?
   In each case give reasons for your view.
   East Anglian Examinations Board

Sex and Marriage

1. a: What did Jesus teach about divorce?
   b: Briefly state *one* argument supporting the practice of divorce and *one* argument against. Do not repeat what Jesus said.
   London Regional Examining Board
2. Turn to the following passages in the New Testament. Ephesians Chap. 5 verses 22 – 26 and Chap. 5 verse 33 to Chap. 6 verse 4.
   a: What is St. Paul's teaching about the attitude that should be shown in a Christian home by:
      (i) husbands to their wives,
      (ii) wives to their husbands,
      (iii) parents to their children,

(iv) children to their parents?

b: Now state your own ideas about the responsibilities and attitudes that are required for a successful marriage.

c: What relationship would you expect to find between parents and children in a happy home?

North Western Secondary School Examinations Board

3. From a Christian point of view, what points can be made in favour of:
   a: a wedding in church.
   b: a period of formal engagement.
   c: chastity before marriage.
   State any opposing arguments which a Christian might make.

   East Anglian Examinations Board

4. Either a: (i) Some families break up. Explain the processes that can cause such a thing to happen.
   (ii) Can you suggest any Christian teaching which might have helped to prevent the break-up?

   OR b: (i) It is sometimes heard, "Marriages are made in Heaven". What What do you think this statement means?
   (ii) What do you think makes for a deeply satisfying marriage?

   Southern Regional Examination Board

Religion

1. a: 'I prayed once, but I never got what I asked for. I never pray now.'
   b: 'When I pray I feel warm and comfortable inside because I have done the right thing.'
   c: 'When I pray I talk to God as a friend and he helps me.'
   d: 'I pray to find out what God wants me to do, and I try to do it.'
   State which of these are in your opinion nearest to true prayer and give your reasons. Try to make your own definition of prayer.

   East Midland Regional Examinations Board

2. "Of course I'm a Christian", said George. "Actually I'm a member of St. Michael's, but I don't go very often – only to the Carol Service at Christmas".
   a: Why do you think George does not go to church more often?
   b: Why does he go to the Carol service?

c: Why does he still want to be thought of as a Christian?
Think of several possible reasons.

East Anglian Examinations Board

3. Either a: (i) Why do you think the church should be involved in the community?
    (ii) Discuss the most effective ways the church works locally.
   OR   b: What do you believe the church should be doing with regard to:
    (i)   Lonely old people.
    (ii) Young people at a loose end.
    (iii) Wives and mothers tied to the home.

Southern Regional Examination Board

4. Write an account of the most important things Christians believe. Which of these things seem to you to give us most help in modern life?

London Regional Examining Board

Index

A
Absenteeism, in industry, 40
Adi Granth, 85
Africaners, 31
Aid to Third World, 12
Alcoholism, statistics, 59, 64
Amnesty International, 72
Anarchy, 67
Arapesh tribe, 3
Aristotle, on leisure, 64

B
'Beatles', The, 89
Birkett, Lord Justice on violence, 54
Black Power, 30
Brandt, Willy, 10
Bristol riots, 47
Britain's help to the Commonwealth, 13
Browning, Robert, on old age, 8
Buddhism, 23, 51, 85, 89

C
Christian Aid, 13
Civil servants, number in Britain, 66
Clarke, Charles, 87
Communism, 2, 67, 71, 73, 85
Confucius, 67

D
Democracy, 68
Dresden, bombing of, 47

E
Ellwood, Wayne, 16

F
'Flanders Fields', 46

G
Gandhi, 30, 74
General Election 1979, how people voted, 69
Germany, Nazi, 1
Grenfell, Wilfred, 41
Gross National Product, 16

H
Handfasting, 78
Heath, Edward, 10
'Hidden Persuaders, The', 20
Hinduism, 85
Hiroshima, 47
Hitler, 1
'Homelands', 33
Hooliganism, 47, 57
Huddleston, Trevor, 44

I
International Voluntary Service, 14
'Internationalist, The', 16
Islam,
  levy for the poor, 25
  war, 51
Israel, kibbutzim, 2

J
Jackson, Jesse, 31
Jesus,
  as a child, 6
  and family life, 6
  and war, 52
  and government, 72
  and marriage, 79
Jesus Movement, 91
Jews,
  and war, 52
  in Russia, 72
  in Palestine, 2
  and home life, 6
Johnson, General, U.S.A. and Vietnam, 54
Jung, Dr. on mental health, 87

K
Kelvin, Lord, 91
Kennedy, John F, 10
Kibbutzim in Israel, 2
King, Dr. Martin Luther, 30
Koran, the, 85
Kreisler, Fritz, 23
Kruschev, on nuclear war, 47

L
Lennon, John, 89
Li Urh, 67
Lincoln, Abraham, 30
Lloyd George, David, 46
Local Government officers, Number in Britain, 66

M
Maharishi Marash, 89
Malnutrition, 9
Massachusetts Institute of Technology, analysis of food scarcity, 10
Marx, Karl, 67, 70
Mead, Margaret, 3
Miami riots, 51
Mohammed and war, 49
Mundugumor tribe, 3

N
National Association for Mental Health, 87
Nazism, 1

O
Opinion Research Centre on leisure activities, 63
Oxfam, 13

P
Packard, Vance, 'The Hidden Persuaders', 20
Paul, St., on money, 19
Pregnancies before marriage, 79
Pyrrhus, the soldier king, 23

Q
Quakers and war, 52

R
Refugees, 16
Russell, Bertrand, on boredom, 38
Russia, children in, 2

S
Shaw, Bernard, on leisure, 59
South Africa, race problem, 31
Soweto, 31
Sparta, 1
Stewart Smith, D.G. Casualties under Communism, 71

T
Taylor, Peter, on absenteeism in industry, 40
'The Queen' interviewing students, 19
'Towards International Co-operation', 27
Turin riots, 51

U
UNESCO and malnutrition, 9
United Nations
  and World Poverty, 12
  and Human Rights, 51
Universal Declaration of Human Rights, 51
U.S.A. race problem, 30

V
Venereal diseases, 78
Voluntary organisations, 13, 14
Voluntary work, 14

W
Wealth, distribution in Britain, 19
Welfare State, 74
Wesley, John, on money, 26
Wilson, Woodrow, 46
Women's Liberation Movement, 42
World Bank, 16